# Why I Chase Comedians

## And Other Bipolar Tales

ISBN 978-1-914603-08-2 (Paperback)
ISBN 978-1-914603-09-9 (Epub ebook)
ISBN 978-1-914603-10-5 (Adobe ebook)

Illustrations on pages xv–xvi by Amber Jefferson: www.amberpip.co.uk

All royalties from the sale of this book go to support the Read and Grow Society (see panel at the end of the book) helping disadvantaged people to learn to read.

Printed by Severn, Gloucestershire, UK.

Main UK distributor: Gardners Books, 1 Whittle Drive, Eastbourne, East Sussex, BN23 6QH. Tel: +44 (0)1323 521777; sales@gardners.com; www.gardners.com

North American distribution: Ingram Book Company, One Ingram Blvd, La Vergne, TN 37086, USA. Tel: (+1) 615 793 5000; inquiry@ingramcontent.com

A catalogue record can be obtained from the British Library.

Ebook: *Why I Chase Comedians And Other Bipolar Tales* is available as an ebook and also under library subscription models.

Published 2022 by:
Waterside Press
Hook, Hampshire, United Kingdom.
Telephone +44(0)1256 882250
Online catalogue WatersidePress.co.uk
Email enquiries@watersidepress.co.uk

# Why I Chase Comedians

### And Other Bipolar Tales

Frankie Owens

**W WATERSIDE** PRESS

# Contents

## Publisher's note

The views and opinions in this book are those of the author and not necessarily shared by the publisher. Readers should draw their own conclusions concerning the possibility of alternative views or accounts. Some names, places and descriptions have been changed.

## Introduction and acknowledgements

I wish to emphasise that although based on what has happened in my life some details may have been altered, especially where these concern people or places. Household names apart, many passages have been fictionalised. Accounts of my bipolar or other episodes may describe distortions of thinking but that's the whole point of writing this book. If you lead a normal life, then you only have normal stories.

My heartfelt thanks to the people I have met that inspired me to write about them. But who gets the most thanks? This is like the eternal question, 'Which came first the Egg or the Chicken?' or 'Why do washing machines eat socks?' I've decided that the most thanks go to my publisher Bryan Gibson. He's given many writers who have slipped through the cracks of civil society a voice that would never have been heard. The Waterside press mission statement 'Putting justice into words' is not just a tagline, it's a heartfelt sentiment of this honourable publishing house.

My special thanks also go to Amber Jefferson for the two contrasting images at the start of the book.

And to you my readers.

Frankie Owens
April 2022

## About the author

Frankie Owens III is a mental health survivor. He was diagnosed with bipolar disorder hypermania ten years ago after serving a prison sentence. Remarkably, after publishing his acclaimed work *The Little Book of Prison* (2012) and lecturing to criminologists and students in colleges and universities across the UK, on April Fools' Day 2020 he again hit the headlines and found himself back in prison after a manic episode.

His writing has been featured in *The Guardian*, *Huffington Post* and *Royal Society For the Arts Journal* and he is the founder of the Read and Grow Society (2013) that teaches disadvantaged people to read and develop their literacy skills. *Why I Chase Comedians* is his attempt to convey the debilitating impact of mania and associated states of mind.

This book is dedicated to the one in four people who suffer a mental health challenge. Celebrate your unique abilities in your condition, as you have some very special talents. There are two dates in your life — the day you were born and the day you realise what you're on the planet to do. I hope very much that you find that second date soon.

Also to Martin William Staton (*Chapter 5*). Whoever made him created a masterpiece, an infectious spirit who filled our hearts with mischief and laughter, generosity and kindness. 'Anger' made the world a better place.

## What the experts say

'Frankie Owens is an excellent person to give insight into the turmoil associated with mental illness.

Without the gremlins in his background, he is always charming and energetic but there have been occasions in his life (some described in the book) where his world has been turned upside down uncontrollably by episodes of mental illness.

Never have I had a stranger call as his GP than when he was found raging in a boating pond on the South Coast of England without much clothing on (which he mentions in *Chapter 2*), so from there things could only get worse.

As always Frankie turns these episodes to good use and is always looking at ways of helping other sufferers and families caught in the network of mental illness. Hopefully *Why I Chase Comedians* will receive the attention and success it deserves.'

*Dr Colin Turner GP*

'Frankie Owens never fails to deliver a no-punches-pulled account of mental health and his time spent at Her Majesty's pleasure. Students soak up his stories, told with characteristic raw honesty and humour.'

*Dr Tim Turner, Assistant Professor, School of Psychological,*
*Social and Behavioural Sciences, Coventry University*

'We know that there are many mental health challenges in the prison environment, and they convey many into its walls. But we know little about how aspects of mental health actually lead to them becoming incarcerated, or what it is like to be in prison and suffer from poor mental health, with meagre access to appropriate services.

This great, accessible book takes us on a journey revealing the reality of being bipolar, and its interfaces with incarceration.

We know we need to open-up insights into the prison environment to address social injustices in our society. This is the reason *Why I Chase Comedians* helps in gaining an understanding of the impact of mental health in prison, and it gives us important social insights into how some uniquely cope with it.'

*Dr Paul Norman, Head of the School of Criminology*
*and Criminal Justice, University of Portsmouth*

'Frankie Owens visited Bangor University to speak to our Criminology and Criminal Justice students about his *Little Book of Prison*. He told his story with honesty and great critical insights into the failings of our prison and rehabilitation systems.

Our students were captivated by his experiences and his passion for Read and Grow, the community literacy programme that he started.'

*Martina Feilzer, Professor Criminology and*
*Criminal Justice, University of Bangor*

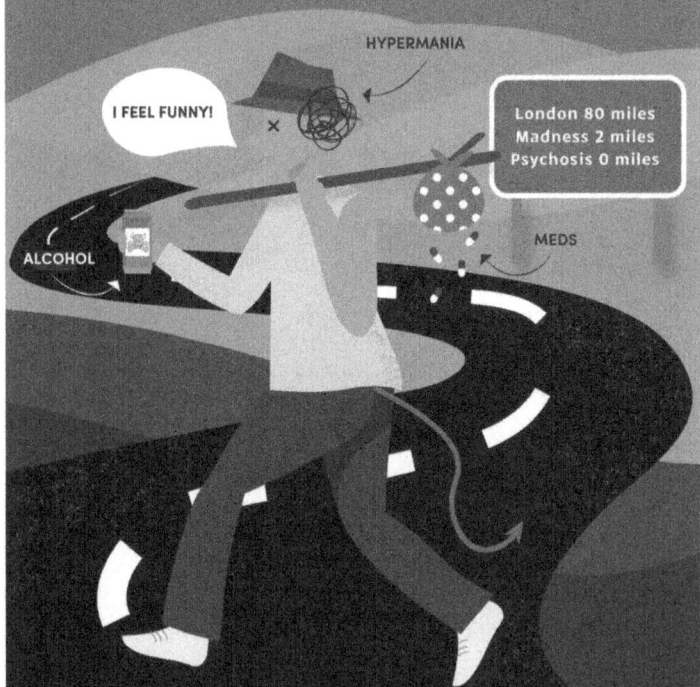

# Chapter 1

'Wait for Me Funny Man!'

---

I'd been manic for weeks. Now I'd gone into another episode, which is not good, ever. It had been an interesting night, I got home in the early hours, popped my medication and was off to the Land of Nod. Next morning I nipped round to Dad's and shouted the usual, 'Ola.' But he was fuming and yelled to me in his Everton accent.

'What the hell have you been doing, you idiot?!'

'What? Nothing!'

'You're in all the bloody papers you cretin!' he raged at me as I started to put the kettle on.

'What you on about?'

He'd heard from my uncle that *The Sun* and *The Mirror* both had a story about a well-known comedian who'd been caught-up in a 'ROAD RAGE HORROR.' The troublemaker was me.

I'd come down from the episode but was still manic. In mania you're defensive and your mind functions on another level. I had full recollection of the night before, but in my bipolar brain no-one got hurt (or arrested) so what was the problem? I explained this in a blasé way, which made Dad even more angry.

'You were on The Camp, you got thrown out … It looks like they want to press charges!'

'For what? … I went to see the cabaret and was told to leave, so I did! Anything else was well off of The Camp so what's it got to do with them?'

'What the bleedin' hell did you do it for in the first place?'

He started quoting from the news story (or a combination of the two red tops' 'EXCLUSIVES'). So I calmly said, 'Come on Dad, don't believe everything you read in the papers, you know they lie.' I have to say I was impressed at how the story made that morning's papers. That was serious PR-speed. Dad continued his rant.

'So, you didn't blah blah blah…'

'OK, yeah, I did! But it's all out of context! All I wanted to do was hand him my script, but his driver sped off. So I followed them!' In my bipolar brain this had seemed perfectly reasonable.

'Yeah, you damn well did! But for 80 bloody miles?'

I'd made the national press years before… as a hero… but this time I was well and truly the villain. Dad sat shaking his head with a look of sheer disbelief on his face, but also deeply worried for my mental health. To him (and evidently the STAR and his driver) these were obviously not the actions of a *normal* person… Well, all three had a point there.

### Plan A

So, to take a step back, I was told that a famous comedian was appearing on The Camp as the STAR attraction and that no leisure members (me included) or staff were allowed over the ballroom to see the show. Now, technically I was a leisure member, although my direct debit had bounced the last few months as I was skint. And to be fair, I'd never heard of this STAR before, but I was told he was getting paid a huge sum and figured someone that good would be worth meeting and handing my script to.

Turns out he's a northern lad, like our lot—but Manchester not Liverpool. I wasn't going to hold that against him as long as he was blue. I grew up on the camps and saw some of the great STARS like Bob Monkhouse, Jim Bowen, Jimmy Tarbuck, Charlie Williams, Mick Miller, Jethro and the late, great Frank Carson ... he was my favourite. In the old days they would come over to the show bar afterwards, they'd meet the guests and have a drink with the general manager ... That was my Dad. There'd be loads of banter and my old man was always the funniest! The more he drank, the funnier he got. He was my comedy hero.

One time Mick Miller was on stage and my uncle was heckling from the audience. He was getting more laughs than the STAR and after ten minutes Mick came over and offered him the microphone — gracious, humble, enjoying the crack. In the old days the STAR would also stay over for breakfast and sign autographs and have photos taken with the punters.

I asked if this STAR was staying overnight but nope, he does the show, pockets his large fee and he's offski — DENIED! See, had he been staying over I could have met him, told him how great he was and how much I liked his show then handed him my script — but it was not to be. I had to come up with a Plan B.

### Plan B

I went into the leisure club and sat in the steam room hatching my plan. I had on my pink three-piece suit and a trilby, which I figured would be so overt it would be covert — 'If it's good enough for Gatsby then it's good enough for me,' I thought. The leisure club closed at 9 pm and the STAR was on at 9.30. I asked a member of staff for a blackboard marker and I drew on cartoon-sized eye lashes and a big moustache. I was going for eccentric, cartoonish and larger than life. Plan B was to get through security, watch and heckle — as a gentleman not a showkiller — then approach him afterwards with the script.

In this attire I hoped it would intrigue him just enough.

I got into the show without any problems and sat close enough to listen to his act which was going down well enough. I wanted a drink but couldn't risk going to the bar as I'd get noticed: first *I'm not allowed* in the cabaret bar and second *I'm skint,* so would have to blag the drink ... I opted to go to the motor to get a can instead. On coming back in I was caught by security,

'Frankie ... I thought that was you! Nice suit! .... But sorry mate the general manager has seen you and you have to leave.'

'No problem, John boy,' I replied to this lovely lad, a friend of the family, 'I just wanted to meet him and give him my script.'

### Plan C

It was time for Plan C. Once, when I was in my twenties (two-and-a-half decades ago) Frank Carson was *the* STAR cabaret. He was, shall we say, well lubricated for social intercourse and put on a brilliant act — as always, it was A CRACKER! Afterwards he was in the show bar on the whisky with the guests. What a character, what a legend! The fastest wit in the world. Well, I was manic, but way before my bipolar diagnosis, so I shouted across from the far end of the room.

'Mr Carson, Mr Carson ... you're the best!'

My voice can be loud for my mid-size frame (think Brian Blessed). Frank raised his whisky glass with a smile.

'Mr Carson, please, please, let me buy you a drink?'

'Go on, Son!' came his slurred reply.

I ordered a double Jamesons, but as usual I was potless so I blagged the barmaid. Then I fought through his fans and came up beside him, handed over his bevy and shouted, 'A toast to Mr Carson!' Everyone cheered and I announced, again over loudly and above the chatter, 'I want to thank you, Mr Carson, I've never made so much money as I have with you … You're the best jockey ever!'

Frank Carson's eyes went weird, and he bit! I have always observed that the best of the best STARS *never* lose their cool. He said, 'I'm Frank Carson, not Willie!' For those readers who cannot picture the two Carsons you would have to be ten times more lubricated than Frank was to ever, ever, think that one could be mistaken for the other. I shouted, 'Love you Willie,' gave him a bear hug and everyone cracked up. They, like me, thought it was a good gag.

I walked back to where I'd been standing, met my pal, blagged a bevy and got him to pay for Frank's drink too! The next few hours were priceless. Every few minutes me and my pal would lift our glasses and shout across the room, 'To Willie' and beam across at him. He would grin back and raise his glass, too. What a STAR! He *loved* the crack. To be fair we did take it too far in the end.

Back in the old days there was a camp photographer known as 'Frank the Flash' who would take pictures of the STAR with guests, which would be processed overnight and be on display at breakfast by the entrance to the restaurant. With my pal I strolled across to work, hung-over but buzzing from the previous night's giggle. We went to walk into the restaurant and Flash boy grabbed us.

'You numbskulls!'

'What's up, Frank?'.

'Look what you pair of tossers have done! I've not sold a single photo! You wrecked every one.'

Turns out we'd invented photo bombing. I swear, every shot had us in the background with caps and sticks doing jockey moves. MATE, we wet ourselves, apologised and went to graft—I've always found it easier to ask forgiveness than ask permission—just another giggle at The Camp office.

To this day I've still no idea where we got those caps from.

Over the years I was offered, by entertainments managers on the camps, to become a greencoat. I always said the same thing, 'I'm overqualified.' I wasn't, of course, but I *was* earning more as a waiter (what with tips) entertaining my allotted 35 diners, three shows a day, dressed in a bow tie but not in the spotlight.

So on with plan C. I changed my clothes, rubbed-off the black marker and figured I'd around an hour before the STAR finished his set. I knew his journey would mean that he had to leave down one particular road. I decided I'd create a roadblock and so I drove down to the village—where there was a load of barriers stacked-up from some recent roadworks—and I lobbed a few, together with a stop sign, into the back if my estate car. It was a race against time…

Now, one of my favourite writers is the late, great John Sullivan of 'Only Fools and Horses' fame even though some people claim he nicked the idea. As Ronnie Wood of the Rolling Stones says, 'It's not what you steal but how you steal it'—and John (if he really did that) did it beautifully. He grew-up in working-class London (no silver spoon) and wrote about what he knew, which was wide boys and market men. He kept on writing scripts and sending them to the BBC and they kept being rejected, but John kept going. He was a hustler. He got a job at the Beeb as a props man—he knew it was a step closer to the powers that be. He used to 'borrow' scripts and learned how to write them so that they were 'telly ready.' One day he was in the canteen and John's mate said to him, 'That's Ray Butt.'

'Who's he?' says John.

'He's the man associated with "Till Death Us Do Part." He's hot stuff.'

When Ray went home John followed him and when finally Ray went into a pub John strolled up to him and said, 'Ray, can I buy you a drink … to celebrate?'

'Celebrate what?' says Ray.

John beamed, 'Because we're going to be working together!'

'Really, on what?'

John smiled, 'I don't know, I haven't written it yet!'

John took a gamble and with big risks come big rewards.

So, my road barrier was fully assembled and it looked pretty convincing. I then went back to The Camp to look for any evidence of the driver to the STAR. I thought he'd defo be a pound in front and would have a driver. YES, MATE! There was a Merc parked by the stage door with a guy reading the paper. I went back to my roadworks, script in hand and manic bipolar brain in overdrive, trying to come up with my intro. I will admit I was starting to get nervous, which is not good when you're manic, TRUST! A man with money is no match for a hypermanic bipolar man on a mission.

It was pitch black and I had my headlights on; I was also now dressed in black but still wearing my trilby. The van came down the road, and it was 'SHOW TIME!' It stopped and the STAR didn't even look up—he was on a laptop.

'Yes, mate?' came a northern sounding voice from the direction of the driver.

'Do you have any jump leads?' Not my best line I have to admit.

'No,' came the answer, with a look of 'What's going on here?'

I went to the car to grab my script. Meanwhile, the driver took off over the plastic feet of my roadblock and was on his way. Now, if that had been a scene from 'Only Fools and Horses' it would have been hilarious. To me it was a red rag to a hypermanic bull—what if I'd really been stranded? The driver was rude, unhelpful, and worst of all kiboshed my Plan C. My mania tipped over into mayhem. I was turning to the dark side.

## Plan D

A gentleman knows where the line is drawn and never crosses it, a cad knows where the line is drawn and constantly does so. Comedians are always taking risks. Some ideas work and some don't. But you never know until you try. I'd failed and the wheels had come off Plan C—well and truly off. Plan D was now in full effect and I was bending the steering wheel for all I was worth. Well, as TV quizmaster Bradley Walsh says, 'The chase is on!' and a full-blown episode was set in motion at speeds beyond all limits.

You can read the headlines. I'm not going through all the ins-and-outs. I'm neither proud of what transpired nor happy with how it made the STAR or his driver feel. I'm ashamed of my bipolar behaviour and Dad was right—I'd behaved like a mammoth idiot, a real dick head and was truly sorry for going over the edge of reason—too far, in fact, by around 80 miles there and 80 miles back. A hypermanic cad (in episode) is different gravy, TRUST!

I'm not asking for forgiveness, just a little understanding or (at least) an audience to the context of my mental health condition—you can be the judge. It wasn't the victims that were at fault it was me … But in my bipolar state I was being misunderstood.

So back home Dad was still going mad, and I was being a cad, manic style.

'Hold on, Dad, by the time I got back it was in the early hours! How did this end up in the Sunday papers?' I tried and failed to give him some warped logic and perspective on this shameful event. 'Dad, there are atrocities across the globe, rapists, paedophiles in church cloth, people in poverty, homelessness and crimes against humanity! Why is this such a sensational and worthy piece of must read news?' Well, I hadn't actually seen the news, so I told Dad I'd look at it for myself, listen to the STAR's radio show and then come back to see him. Outside of the manic episode I wasn't angry, but I was disappointed that Plan D had failed. I apologised to Dad and realised that it had been a very, very bad day at the bipolar office. Life goes on, though and the world keeps turning. I had one wheel left on my wagon and I was still rolling. Was I one of the top ten most wanted and most heinous criminals on the planet? I thought not. Had Lucifer reserved a special place in Hell for me? Unlikely.

Well, it wasn't just two national newspapers that the story ended up in, it was more like ten. Words like 'HORROR' and 'FEARED FOR HIS LIFE' were being headlined and gobbled up by the masses. Yep, my script could have given him a lethal paper cut!

I listened to the STAR's radio show and heard his take on the misadventure. He and his guest, another comedian, were making some good gags and I particularly liked the Rutger Hauer reference ... 'Great actor.' What was interesting was that the STAR said he wasn't pressing charges as no crime had been committed. He was also thinking of using the experience as material for a new show. So, ultimately, out of a negative came some real positives. The STAR got some BIG NATIONAL PR, so did The Camp and it looked as if nothing more would happen to me.

So, I said, 'Great news, Dad, he's not pressing charges ... get in there! "Get out of jail free card!"' I apologised again to him and went off on another (mis) adventure. It's well over two years ago now and I'd like to try and explain how my bipolar episodes manifest themselves. Maybe then you might be able to make a little more sense of such a nonsensical event? You might not, but don't worry because if you *do* understand then you're probably just as sane as I am!

As for myself, I'll continue to reach for the moon, miss, and be amongst a STAR or two. 'There's no business like showbusiness ...'

# Chapter 2

Welcome to My Bipolar World

---

If you've met one person with bipolar, then you've met one person. Every sufferer is affected differently by this condition…TRUST! My own mania is when I'm most risk to myself and the people I meet (especially in full-blown hypermanic episodes). There is a difference between manic, which is euphoric (and I have to say great fun) and the next level, where you detach from reality and behaviour is way, way beyond eccentric.

### Living on the edge

Being bipolar and manic is like living on the edge. Your adrenaline increases, your endorphins are released faster (and in bigger quantities), your muscles feel stronger, your cardio is better and best of all your brain is higher functioning. It is as if you are naturally high because of your condition. You start to access more information from your brain's memory banks and your state is semi-hypnotic. Your senses of smell and touch are heightened, you can hear from greater distances and music and literature become joyful experiences as if they'd been written *just for you*. Who wouldn't want to feel like that?

In mania, my core values and beliefs are still intact. I try to help people, entertain, and give as much as I can to anyone looking for help. Isn't that what we are on the planet to do? To help each other and support our communities? Or is it to amass as much wealth as possible, look down our noses at anyone with less than ourselves, and feel bitter when others taste anywhere near the kind of success we've achieved? (Some of these people must be money-mad... a condition that I think is one of the ugliest).

## That Friday feeling

A hypermanic episode can be a momentous experience. As I said you are living on the edge—let's call it a cliff edge. For me, mania does not often lead to hypermania, thankfully. Usually, it passes then I come back down to normality—I return to what is perceived as *normal*. So, I'll try to explain the journey in a way that everyone can make some sense of. Here goes...

Nearly everyone can understand a 'Monday mood'—you've been living it up, loving life, having a great time and enjoying yourself outside the bubble of confusion that is work (and the rat-race). Next thing you know it is Monday again and time to get back to work! Now, as the week progresses, you start to slowly drop your Monday mood and head towards a fantastic Friday feeling instead. When Friday hits, you're well and truly ready to get out and embrace the world again—you're high on life and set to go! Well, mania is like getting from Monday to Friday then feeling like each new day is another Friday. Each Friday then takes you a little higher and this feeling is repeated and enhanced. It's a trigger of the condition and you do become mindful of this, but I personally exercise more and ensure I take my medication at the same time each evening, to help maintain my level of Fridays. My meds are slow-release tablets and, on occasions, when Fridays are coming on in whole weeks, I will adjust my dosage after consulting with my GP.

On this journey it is crucial to not binge on stimulants of any variety, which is difficult when you have an excessive personality. My medication is called Quetiapine (Q), a sophisticated pharmaceutical, which is primarily an anti-psychotic that also contains a strong sedative. Sleep is one of the corner-stones of attempting to achieve good mental wellbeing. But my condition is fluid, never constant, and it is not like having Type 2 diabetes. Q is not like insulin, which controls a physical condition. Q is a substance, a building block to give you a foundation to manage your condition.

I hope I haven't lost you! To explain this can be difficult for a healthcare professional, let alone a normal person who has never had anyone close to them with bipolar. The only people that really, fully comprehend it are those with a mental health condition themselves, which is one-in-four in society. When mania turns into hypermanic episodes it is like teetering on the edge — you leave solid ground but instead of falling off it you fly up into the stratosphere! The higher you go, the more Fridays you meet, the more detached you become, the more likely you are to go into psychosis

## Back to Earth

It's funny how falling feels like flying for a little while. Being in psychosis is like being hypnotised, but it also gives great gifts, extra-sensory perception (ESP), natural language processing (NLP) and hypnotic ability are all possible but not controlled in any way, which can be frighting for all parties. The actor Stephen Fry used to say that he didn't want to take his medication for fear it would rob him of his creativity and that would be criminal, FACT! Frank Bruno the boxer used to say he only wanted to take his medication if he felt unwell. I love, love, love Frank Bruno but I'm afraid that if you wait that long then it is already too late in my humble opinion, 'Know what I mean Harry.'

After a full-blown episode in psychosis, you eventually come back down to Earth like plane, train and car collisions combined. Then you and your loved ones have to deal with the wreckage, the havoc, the fallout, the apologies to the people affected by your performance and occasionally a police officer, judge or newspaper.

I can stand up and say that not even prison can rob me of my creativity. My most recent episode, ironically on April 1, led me to incarceration — guess who's the April Fool now? I'd had an eye-patch made and was deluded in the belief that by wearing it I would be protected from hypnotism, which was some warped logic right there! I was not in full control of my mind, body or actions but ultimately had to face the consequences. I genuinely believed that pirates had two eyes but covered-up one of them to battle the supernatural on the high seas. A little Sinbadesque. You usually find an eye-patch on powerful heroes and villains, or so my bipolar brain was telling me. 'Why are pirates called pirates ... because they AAARRRGGGHHHHH!!'

I'd had some business cards printed at the start of Mad March, while in mania, showing an image of an eye (set in a pyramid) and the word for the Devil (in Muslim) but with no contact details and was giving these out to people as calling cards. In the Muslim religion the Devil is a mere reflection, a shadow of God or the Son of God. His dark side. In my non-manic mind, I defo believe there is good and bad in all of us, but I truly believed in my hyper-manic state that I was in danger of turning to the dark side. Explaining this to you, venting it on the page, is a mixed blessing — or is it a poison chalice? When my brain rebalances or is on its way back down, I can access parts of episodes, fragments, like dreams but rarely see the full picture. My actions and behaviour usually project as intimidating, frightening and nonsensical but never violent. I do not believe there is any pleasure in hitting, hurting or being hit by someone, even while in an episode ... I do hope that this is because these values are at my very core where not even psychosis can unlock them.

## A Norse god rescuing the populace

I was projecting what can only be described as a fantasy role. When arrested by armed police I announced myself as a Norse god explaining that I'd transcended human form and was over 2,000 years old, a traveller and a Bedouin. I was here on Earth, a place I didn't understand. I was here to decide who would live and who would die of COVID! The pandemic had been a massive trigger for me, along with Radio 4 overload alongside days with no medication, no sleep and misuse of an anti-anxiety drug called Baclofen. All these factors had sent me beyond the stratosphere and into the bipolar universe.

Psychiatrists sometimes ask questions about delusions of grandeur, connections with God or God-like feelings or thinking, while holding onto their clipboards, wearing their lab coats. So, reading *Dante's Inferno* and Freud is a bad combination for me, along with my masters' degree. The counter arguments usually infuriate the medical powers that be, undermine their diagnoses and belittle their position of authority. My argument is deflective, loud and cutting. 'Trust me I'm a doctor' doesn't often ring true to my hypermanic brain ... Trust who? ... What? ... Like Harold Shipman?

It is said there is a fine line between genius and madness ... I do not believe I am either. Challenging medics' authority with grandiose rhetoric is a fool's errand. So, let's define *normal* shall we? Or, as I see it — *ordinary*. For once I am speechless so let me ask:

- Are sufferers of mental health disorders a product of environment or is their environment a product of ourselves?
- Are mental health disorders created by the modern civilised world or do they land on us from outer space?
- Is it nature, nurture or the world and our perceived place in it that does not make sense to me and my fellow sufferers?

## Naked in a kayak

When in my non-manic mind, looking at the Western society I live in, we have rules, structures, law and order. If we deviate from these then it's a *dis*order, a *mal*function. If society has order, then why do one in four people within it have mental health disorders? Why does such a huge percentage of society feel they don't belong because they don't conform or comply (and ultimately can't function) within its constraints? Interesting debate, but personally I don't have any answers, only questions and the medication to help me to conform and to function appropriately.

So, April Fools' Day last year had some serious, liberty-taking, fallout consequences. The law and order system felt I should be where law-abiding citizens are not. I was no longer in civil society but being held at Her Majesty's pleasure.

It's the second coming for me. Nine years ago, I suffered the same 'travesty of justice,' meaning because of my mental health. On that occasion, in one episode, I was found naked in a kayak off the South Coast of England, that I'd used without asking its owner. Hardly the actions of a normal person. Nor would you agree of a master criminal? I am clear that both times—during the nude fiasco or the more recent road rage delusion—I was a Norse god. The fault was mine but quite definitely without malice or guilty intent (I would say that wouldn't I though?).

Always turn a negative into a positive. When life gives you lemons, make lemonade. On my first prison sentence I wrote the award-winning *Little Book of Prison: A Beginners Guide* to help first-time offenders, their families and loved ones left behind. It led to me setting up the Read and Grow Society to help ex-offenders and disadvantaged people learn to read. I found out, whilst in the system, that 48 per cent of prisoners could *not* read. Forgive me but if you can't read then what the heck are your choices in life? How can you be an included member of society and your local community? Imagine if you have a mental health issue PLUS you can't read? Surely its game over? Read and Grow is now in its seventh year, giving people the lifelong gift of reading. It is an honour to meet these brave people and help them achieve their dream of literacy when society has failed them and no-one else will help. The system has let them fall into the illiteracy crevasse — to my mind an unforgivable act. I say more about this in *Chapter 10*.

'Will I be back inside every nine years?' I ask myself. Sentence No. 2 began after the system ignored a pre-sentence report that recommended a non-custodial sentence; disregarded a psychiatrist's report that gave a nine-year history of bipolar disorder; and a thick pile of character references ranging across my GP, experts in Criminology and my MP (a member of Boris' Cabinet). All of these were given little to no consideration. Well, how's your luck?!

There are an estimated 30,000 prisoners with mental health disorders currently, in this country — that's one in three of the prison population, incarcerated in an alternative society. I say that to illustrate the opposite of a civil society which I was deemed unfit to be among. Prisoner mental health statistics are shocking and sadly, nine years on from my first stay I fear that nothing has changed in terms of the healthcare provision in Her Majesty's prisons … which continues as before, and that I experienced during my second stay. Added to which we have the biggest prison suicide rate in all of Europe and the highest our system has seen since records began — as well as … wait for it … add to this … COVID incarceration! Twenty-three hours a day in prison lockdown, bang-up! No visits, no gym, no trips to the library, no education classes! I think the phrase we are all looking for here rhymes with 'clucking bell'!

Ultimately, if my mental health condition means that every nine years I have to serve a sentence then I WILL live with that. Some people's mental health is in constant chaos on a daily, or weekly basis. I'm 99 per cent 'normal', which I am very, very thankful for—TRUST!

So, on this new sentence I could at least fine-tune my sitcom script ready for the next opportunity to hand it to a passing comedian—you didn't really think I was giving up that easily, did you? Have a day off! It's laugh or cry in prison and never a nice place to be, and that's when you're feeling some wellbeing in your world.

Survival anywhere is about depth of character and the mental strength to find hope in just a little part of your mind—a place you didn't know existed until you were sunk in it up to your nuts. In nature it is fight or flight, sink or swim, find a way to focus on a positive future and not dwell in a negative present . . . which way would you go? It is a fifty-fifty chance, but you never know till you know. Well, luckily for me my blue prison mug is not half empty but half full. Yet guess what cell number I'm in . . . Room bloody 101! Jesus . . . Am I dreaming this?!

## Can anybody hear me?

'Success isn't final, failure isn't fatal: it's the courage to carry on that counts.' With a deep breath I take great heart from these words of Winston Churchill. To my way of thinking my prison sentence was a satyr play written in the wreckage of injustice, but that's because I'm clearly mad and no-one in the order of things was listening anyway. I do not feel sorry for myself. I am old enough and ugly enough to accept my fate but I smile as I share with you what Charles Bukowski the German-American poet, novelist, and short story writer once said: 'Some people never go crazy. What truly horrible lives they must lead.'

So now you have some knowledge of my condition. With this wisdom, my fate is in your hands. You may choose to either use this to criticise me, or to understand me (just a little). You have the freedom to decide for yourself — I respect everybody's opinion. I feel harmony with the world only if we all have an even playing field and a two-way street on which to contemplate and listen with equal measure and consideration.

Trouble is, from the inside of a prison wall, as a convicted criminal, your voice is far, far harder to hear by civil society, and even harder to respect … but there you go, as in life.

So how did I end up back at HMP Hotel? Well, that's another bipolar tale of court proceedings, lawyers, judges and others in the system …

# Chapter 3

See You in Court (or by Video Link)

---

So let's get right back to when I faced prison second time around. I have to say the day started out full of hope. The Crown Court hearing was set for 10 am in Court 7 — my lucky number! I arrived in good spirits and good time (as if the COVID Traffic Gods were lending me and my driver a helping hand). The sun came out to wish me well too — not a snowball's chance in Hell!

---

### Ben and Jerry

---

Alarm bells should have sounded when I was told by the helpful gents at the court desk that I was actually in Court 4. However, my learned friend — well, associate (and barrister), whose name was Ben, joined me in the COVID corridor (with its social distancing) sounding positive and upbeat. He greeted me with a courtesy elbow-bump and informed me that Court 4 was a pretty good sign. That the judge was 'in training,' and a colleague of his, a fellow QC (Queen's counsel). I saw this differently. I wondered if a judge at the start of his career might be more likely to be as harsh as possible. I kept this to myself and nodded at Ben's enthusiasm.

Ironically, the judge's name was Jerry. So, Ben-the-barrister, Jerry-the-judge and Frankie-the-felon. It felt a little farcical and the whole experience surreal, but I was not surprised or perturbed, and kick-started 'The Frankie Show' by saying to Ben, 'You look much younger in person, especially with your crown topper.' A crown topper is a grey ceremonial wig and I had only until now met Ben on video-link when he was not wearing it. He looked surprised and raised his eyebrows which lifted the wig as if it had a will of its own.

'Do I really?'

I grinned through my reply, 'No, you look older than Rumpole!' (for younger readers 'Rumpole of the Bailey' is an old TV show about barristers and their old school ties, boozy lunches, chambers and back door deals). Ben's face dropped and his wig went back to sleep. He leaned back in his chair and casually told me what a sensible guy Jerry was, 'A lovely guy.'

Well Jerry must have not got laid the night before, lost his shirt on a share dividend and found out his butler was having it away with his wife, as the sentence he handed down to me was far from lovely.

### Dressed for the part

To rewind a little ... when I arrived at the courts they were covered in scaffolding. I was in a nice Saville Row suit (not my 'lucky suit' as it turned out), fairly expensive reading glasses, and a case on wheels with a handle (my 'just-in-case I'm going away case'). My driver was parking the car and I was following some shapely legs in a business suit, on her mobile phone, discussing the likely outcome of her case. I was hopeful she'd be involved in my hearing as she was very easy on the eye until I overheard the minimum tariff her client was likely to receive. She disappeared through a door in the wall and I followed her to find two gents in uniform with lanyards and ID badges around their necks having a ciggie. I approached them and politely asked, 'Excuse me, chaps how do I access reception, please?'

'Are you a barrister?' one responded.

Now, if I'd been at my playful best I would have gone along with the game, answered 'Yes' and got the gossip on Ben's abilities, but truth be told I was a little nervous and I replied honestly.

'No, I am afraid I'm the accused.'

To which his co-worker replied, 'Really, you're not a barrister?'

I assured them both I wasn't, but thanked them for their kind assumptions. I told you this was a surreal event, all round. I found the other side of the building, where my driver joined me. He told me how much he'd paid for parking—scandalous, but I stayed calm. Something I rarely do with parking charges!

## In the COVID corridor

There in the COVID corridor Ben-the-barrister chatted with me about my guilty plea. He'd done a deal with the Crown Prosecution Service (some ageing QC who specialised in big fraud cases). I'd appeared in court virtually on first appearance when a lady judge, get this … by the name Judy had said that the sentencing hearing would also be by video. I was naïve (and delighted) to hear this, thinking that if it's a video-link sentence it will likely be a community order rather than prison. However, Ben informed me that what she meant was that the lawyers would appear initially via a video-link but then I would have to attend court *in person*.

COVID made cases and courts quite messy, and very different in their delivery of services—just like the rest of the world under lockdown. I asked Ben why I had to attend the hearing and his words sent a shiver down my spine. 'Well, Mr Owens, with the greatest respect (a terrible phrase which means that bad news is coming) you need to attend as there is an outside chance you'll be leaving by another door!' By this he meant the trapdoor of injustice: 'Send him down!'

But that was weeks ago, and I'd ruled it out as a non-runner. Now sitting outside Court 4 Ben assured me that my psychiatrist's report gave compelling mitigating circumstances due to my bipolar disorder, my pre-sentence report from probation recommended a community order (PSR recommendations are almost always followed by the judge) and my character references were 'impeccable.' This was Ben's first time back in a real courtroom since COVID lockdown began and he said it was great to get back to some kind of normality. I was pleased for him, and hopeful, with Ben now able to do his *thing* in person. 'There are nuances that can tip the scales of justice,' I told myself.

I should tell you before I go any further that I'm a guest lecturer at colleges and universities to Criminology, Psychology and Sociology students about the prison system and failing healthcare delivery for those with mental health conditions. So how was my luck? I keep abreast of policy and so I knew the Justice Minister was implementing new guidelines to help judges deal with mental health cases, but also that this wasn't coming into effect till October. Here we were in April still! I didn't feel it made any odds not to share this with Ben as I was more interested in his plan for the next 20 minutes.

We continued to talk in the COVID corridor and Ben gave me some words of inspiration. 'Frankie ... I would be bitterly disappointed if you were to receive a custodial sentence today.'

I gathered my thoughts, took a deep breath, and replied, 'Ben, I assure you, you will not be nearly as disappointed as I will be!'

This line was delivered with a raised eyebrow and wide and surprised eyes whilst looking to the heavens. As I made sense of his rhetoric, I noticed an unmarked door next to Court 4. It opened and a young lady in a crown topper and business suit popped her head out for a second and then popped back inside. I figured it must be the tradesman's entrance. Then, a minute later, she popped her head back out but this time in a Harry Potter gown. I had worn gowns like hers graduating at university when I studied Hospitality, then again years later when I did my masters' degree. She nodded towards Ben.

'Morning Ben, how are you?'

'Good morning, Claire,' he replied, 'I'm well, how are you doing?'

Before she had time to answer I added, 'Good morning, pretty eyes, you couldn't get me a coffee could you? Grab yourself one—I take mine strong, and black, like my women.' This is a gag from the film *Airplane* and I usually get a smile in response, but this was not to be. She ignored me and asked Ben casually, 'Ben, can I ask what the maximum sentence for Charge 7 for Mr Owens is?'

My jaw hit the deck. Turns out that pretty eyes was the prosecution barrister, not numpty-the-fraud guy from the video-link! Well, no-one told me, did they?! MATE, WTF!

'Yes Claire, it carries up to 12 months.'

Claire smiled, 'Thank you, Ben, see you in court.'

She looked at me and retorted, 'Pretty eyes,' all the while looking me up-and-down, from head to toe, then she vanished into the wall as the hidden door closed behind her. I turned to Ben. He was smiling at me, so I shrugged and said, 'Ben, you could have told her it was six months!'

'Yes, I could,' he replied, 'but that would have been dishonest.'

I nodded in defeat thinking about how nice it was to meet an honest barrister—just my luck it's my own. As I said, watch Rumpole, its hilarious with its manipulations and legal trickery, still being repeatedly shown on Yesterday TV. There's a pub in my town called 'The Honest Politician'—but not impossible for either profession in my humble opinion.

In the past, I'd met barristers in my social circle and they all reminded me of John Cleese in 'A Fish Called Wanda' … eccentric, ill-mannered and having affairs left, right and centre. You know, men of means, people of rank and privilege and above all integrity. Here's an insight into this world. A few years ago, a new framework was introduced to allow potential clients to approach barristers directly rather than through a solicitor. I'd often ask how a solicitor decides which barrister they appoint on behalf of their client. One answer, admittedly given over a large brandy, was 'The one that meets you in the car park with the thickest brown envelope.' As in sales, referrals earn a commission, and apparently money makes the world go round. In our very civilised society, with impeccable law and order as far back as Magna Carta, there is justice for all, etc. Just another of my bipolar views!

So direct access meant that you didn't need to cut a deal via the middleman (the solicitor), a solid government initiative giving value to the person in the street. Priceless! Barristers, especially Queens Council (the senior rank, which takes at least ten years of service before you make it up the greasy pole) also had to go on training courses to learn how to speak to the public as many of them didn't know how to converse with ordinary folk, or how much a pint of milk cost.

## One door shuts ...

Now, in my humble opinion there are *two* main types of criminals — the ones that get caught and the ones who don't. Then there are those who are beyond the law like members of the royal family or whose operations are off the scale and maybe hidden behind a business facade, colossal entrepreneurs that steal staff pension funds, and those who manipulate the corridors of power. Those with great power (really meaning money and blackmail tokens) have a built-in 'get out of jail free card' so there has to be really strong law and order to have a civil and inclusive society. I believe the scales of justice can be swayed by delicate influences, ultimately making a mockery of the system and structures we are supposed to follow. Crazy, but true that you are three times more likely to go to prison once you've been inside. What does that say about the delivery of rehabilitation in this country? Nelson Mandela once said, 'A society should not be judged by how it treats its highest citizens rather how it treats its lowest ones.'

I'll sum up my sentencing hearing—it was a HUGE mess, one of the highest order. Grumpy Jerry-the-judge (who, by the way, in my bipolar mind was wearing red high heels, stockings and crotchless under-crackers beneath his desk) ignored common sense by handing down a one-year sentence. It is a cliché to say this was unfair, or unjust, as every prisoner will tell you that, but this really was a MASSIVE travesty of justice and no mistake. My bipolar brain had been level during the pomp and ceremony until the sentence was handed down and, in that moment, it was like being injected with the amphetamine of injustice, an entire year's worth, in one hit! My mind started thinking of my children and my loved ones. 'Send him down!' rang in my ears as I was escorted from the court by (you guessed it!) ANOTHER DOOR!

As we went down the stairs, one of the guards said, 'Well, that was a bloody joke!' I was in complete agreement, but somehow I failed to see the funny side of it. As I was put into my pink-walled holding-cell, I asked the time; it was 11.15 am. In one hour and 15 minutes my life had changed for the very worst. It was becoming an even bigger game of luck under COVID and I didn't feel too clever. I thought I'd contracted a new virus—'unluckiness'—and it would go on to last for six months in prison … the half of my sentence I would actually serve behind bars. I sat on my wooden bunk with a couple of cups of coffee, a crusty tuna sarnie and some old tabloids. Luckily, there were no comedians being chased in these editions as I ran through the pages in slow motion and time stood still. My new situation began to dawn on me. My local HMP was only five minutes away, so I figured I'd be there for lunch at least, but that was not to be. GUTTED.

The cell door opened. The bad news came. 'We're going to another prison, an hour and 40 minutes' drive away as the local prison is overcrowded.' Plus, we had to wait for another hearing to finish in case the defendant was leaving by the same door as me. There was also only one fun bus (prison van) to transport all of us due to COVID. No matter what I would be in the pink pad until late-afternoon at the earliest! Deep joy! Plus it was 28 degrees centigrade outside so the cubicles of the fun bus would be sweat boxes on wheels AND it would turn out to be full so it would take longer for us to get out of that 'loser cruiser' at the prison.

My thoughts as all this dawned on me were, 'Am I dreaming?' I was truly lost for words when Ben appeared at my door. His words were, 'Frankie I am bitterly disappointed at the outcome.' I let them linger, but was gracious in defeat, I told him that he'd done his best and that it was just a very, very bad day at the bipolar office for yours truly.

Ben said we should appeal, and I agreed but knew that COVID lockdown meant that would probably take longer than my sentence. 'It is what it is,' I consoled myself, 'and you are where you are ... the only one to blame is you, yourself and the person sitting in this cell.'

When the time came the traffic was kind and the driver of the fun bus was defo on a promise. The van was over-revving, the air-con broken and he had the heating on FULL BLAST to keep the engine cool. Oh the humanity! Eventually, we sat (six of us) in the prison reception area (the 'holding area') awaiting the new prisoner booking in process. The part I really enjoyed was the strip search ... 'Touch your toes' time, a bit like being at public school (I'm told), with the joys of the prisoner's brown, rusty-pocket penetration always an experience where you pray for an officer with short, thin fingers.

As always, I stuck out like a sore thumb in my Saville Row suit. I was surrounded by young men 25 years my junior talking prison slang, and very loudly indeed. In my experience the loudest man in the room is often the weakest man in the room. The topics of conversation were standard stuff.

'This is the worst jail I've ever been to!'

'My judge was a stupid old git and my barrister was worse!'

'I'm getting a single cell, I'll kick the hell out of anyone so I don't have to share!'

And so on, and so on, blah blah blah.

## Another door opens ...

'Go to jail, go directly to jail, do not pass go for six months.' In my, case that is a brutal FACT! Next a quick visit to the nurse; blood pressure fine, temperature fine and I was told there were no COVID cases so far at this HMP Hotel. Good to know. One other piece of good news was that my medication was safely in the nurses' possession. Lack of medication was one of the factors that led to this accommodation and without it in this environment things could get very dangerous very fast. Then, the news that we were going to a COVID lockdown wing for 14 days' isolation! Well, my cup runneth over.

I was one of the lucky ones as I'd packed three pencils and three writing pads. I would be going 'old skool,' writing for business and for pleasure. I figured this would be a productive sentence for both my mind and my body. A health farm of sorts mixed with a drying-out clinic even though I had been off the drink for five weeks prior to my sentence (or court jester appearance). I was cool, and calm, and collected. In reality, it was a very short sentence when some of the lads were looking at years not months.

As in any walk of life there is always someone less fortunate than yourself. It's impossible not to feel aggrieved, and you can't weigh up the pros and cons equally when you have the court fiasco fresh in your mind. What I *do* know is that prison the second time around was at least a known entity with far less to worry about, only to work through and 'ride out'.

I'm in my single cell and the medication is popped at the medical hatch (as I'm not allowed them in possession until tomorrow). Ah, tomorrow, when my new adventure really begins. There is no doubt that tonight the walls will be closing in and I will dream of giant crown toppers chasing me down a rabbit hole. In my dream I will most certainly be the Mad Hatter, but I wish I could be the Cheshire Cat and simply disappear. I can talk my way out of a room with no doors, but this time my mouth (and bipolar brain) has got me firmly locked-up behind one. Onwards and upwards!

# Chapter 4

Medication … That's What You Need

Roy Castle was the presenter of the 1980s TV show 'Record Breakers.' He used to play the trumpet and sing, 'Dedication, dedication, dedication, that's what you need. If you want to be the best, and if you want to beat the rest, dedication.' Roy, I couldn't agree more but have adapted the lyrics. 'Medication, not dedication.'

It is amazing how tunes and lyrics stay with us and yet knowledge we try to keep in our head is lost. Some of the things we suffer in our lives are of our own making, my body is telling me that yesterday's workout was a bad idea, the lunges have rendered my legs almost useless. My bipolar brain is not of my conscious making, it can be a great servant or a terrible master. This morning it is wired as the heat, severe lack of airflow, noise of mentally-disturbed neighbours and the environment disrupted my usual solid sleep.

### Prison healthcare

I have filled in another app to ask if my meds can be increased from 300mg to 400mg. Fingers crossed they agree to this. My medical notes clearly show a history of nine years of Quetiapine use (Q is a powerful antipsychotic with a strong sedative). If only prison healthcare connected to my local doctor's surgery. Wouldn't that be a novel idea? Sharing crucial information on prisoners' health and mental wellbeing, I would love to know the explanation. It defies belief that each prison governor's compact (a sort of mission statement) professes to deliver 'The same healthcare service as prisoners would receive in society.' I have seen the document with my own eyes and been a victim of prison health — DON'T — care failing to support or function adequately let alone on a par with that in society.

Once I was finally sectioned under the Mental Health Act and diagnosed with a bipolar condition called hypermania, Q was decided by the Director of Psychiatry to be part of my treatment plan. The dosage began at 800mg a day at the start of my recovery and hand-on-heart was scary to experience. It stops your body and your brain in its tracks, you feel mentally and physically disabled. I had felt this way before in my first mental hospital sectioning in the early-1990s when I was held down and injected with Largactil another anti-psychotic, fondly named the 'chemical cosh.'

This experience was far more severe. I had the worst reaction possible, every potential side-effect, even the unlikely side effects chose me. I looked like I'd had a stroke, unable to control my facial muscles, dribbling down out of the corner of my mouth. It brought on seizures and muscle spasms. I felt like I was suffocating, I could hardly breathe. I honestly thought I was going to die. Thankfully it subsided and although I woke-up in a padded cell with a fetching white jacket that had arms that went all the way around the back, I was happy still to be breathing — my body was still spasming and my veins felt like they were filled with hot treacle.

The difference with daily doses of this size and the potency of the pharmaceuticals is that the disability is relentless, it's constant, it goes on for, not weeks, but months. You struggle to hold a bowl of cereal in one hand and finding your mouth with the spoon is like a gastronomic version of pinning the tail on a donkey. It is near on impossible to hold a thought or string a sentence together and the little self-awareness you do have is of a state of panic. You are rendered comatose in a semi-awake state at best, with daily chunks of narcolepsy. I would have perished had I been using heavy machinery.

### A claustrophobic tube

Going through this period of my recovery was a necessary evil to rebalance the receptors in my brain and reduce chemical activity in my hypermanic state. It's common practice in psychiatry and treatment planning for mental health patients but experiencing it feels like the end of the world. It is as if you are crawling in slow motion along a claustrophobic tube (think 'Shawshank Redemption' escape tunnel) that you are told has a light at the end of it. The treatment plan sets out to reach its hopeful outcome in the medium- to long-term; the patient's reality, in the beginning, is a living nightmare that he or she is supposed to be thankful for, scared, alone and in the darkest of places.

At this stage when occasionally self-aware you wonder if this current existence is forever, and if any future 'quality of life' will return or exist again. Nurses tell you how much better you are getting when you feel far worse than the mental-illness you were suffering from before your recovery plan. A poor choice of words, as at this stage you are in a worse mental state than you ever were, better to say, 'You're in a world of pain and suffering but you're not going into episodes or being arrested so that's the main thing.' 'Thank you so much, nurse.'

In truth we are talking about the prevention of 'episodes in psychosis' rather than a cure for a condition/illness/abnormality of the mentally-ill mind. Doctors have studied anatomy for thousands of years, we are pretty much at the top of our game. We can replace organs, we can engineer limbs, insert heart pumps, we can re-attach tissue and cells. But I never understood why we grew an ear on a mouse or why a genetically engineered Dolly the sheep, back in 1986, caused such a moral panic. Dolly was an anatomical success, we cloned improved DNA, she grew bigger and faster, produced double the amount of milk, could grow more wool, all virtues of the three-year project and the brilliance of the pioneering scientists, loads of pros to rolling-out this principle to other livestock. The Achilles' heel was played down and phrased as requiring more care (Dolly's behaviours were abnormal to the nature of her species). They could create the anatomy down to the last strand of DNA, but they had no clue about how to synthesise the evolution cycle into the brain of an animal.

### Psychology, psychiatry, psychopathy…

A species' evolution of inherent knowledge, it seems, cannot be replicated, but producing a salmon in a fish farm is no problem. Expecting it to return to spawning grounds is a behavioural fact we can observe but cannot explain. My humble opinion is that we face the same conundrum with the human brain; we observe and report findings of behaviour but can do little when trying to explain the connection to the human mind as it is metaphysical. Metaphysical studies generally seek to explain inherent or universal elements of reality that are not easily discovered or experienced in our everyday life.

The field of modern-day Psychiatry has a severe lack of REAL expertise on the mind; it is in its embryonic stage at best. We have 100 years of theory versus 2,000 or more years of anatomy. As a mental health patient that makes our treatment experimental, we have evidence of some success from some pharmaceuticals for part of the behavioural problem, but misdiagnosis can be retrograde to the patient.

I studied A-level Psychology failing the exam dismally but was intrigued by the varied interpretations and glaring contradictions that so-called respected experts in their field not only disagreed on, but had completely opposed beliefs about, i.e. reference the same behaviours in their mentally-ill patients in their exploratory studies. It always appeared to me as ego over explanation, something that manifests itself often by those revered and followed.

Why is it that experts in human anatomy have wholesale agreement on the nature of the human body and there is little to none whatsoever when it comes to those who study the human mind? Unless you are mentally-ill you cannot wholly understand that condition, you must live it. Imagine if learning from experience educated the experts to the degree that they became the students not the teachers. You could create a dystopia where the lunatics ran the asylum — if the experts believe it then the layman soon follows, then the masses are turned to sheep or clones of the mind by those that understand and live in madness.

Let's have some fun with this for a second, I'm more than happy to not have all the answers and I don't profess to be an expert of any kind, only someone who routinely survives a mental health condition and lives with it. Read the following information and try to match these behaviours to anyone you know directly, by first-hand experience, or indirectly through balanced media channels. The 'triarchic model' suggests that different conceptions of psychopathy emphasise three observable characteristics to various degrees. Analyses have been made with respect to the applicability of measurement tools such as the Psychopathy Checklist revised (PCL-R) and Psychopathy Personality Inventory (PPI).

- **Boldness** Low fear including stress tolerance, toleration of unfamiliarity and danger, and high self-confidence and social assertiveness. The PCL-R measures this relatively poorly (and mainly through Facet 1 of Factor 1). Similar to PPI fearless dominance. May correspond to differences in the amygdala and other neurological systems associated with fear.
- **Disinhibition** Poor impulse control including problems with

planning and foresight, lacking effect and urge control, demand for immediate gratification, and poor behavioural restraints. Similar to PCL-R Factor 2 and PPI impulsive antisociality. May correspond to impairments in frontal lobe systems that are involved in such control.

- **Meanness** Lacking empathy and close attachments with others, disdain of such attachments, use of cruelty to gain empowerment, exploitative tendencies, defiance of authority, and destructive excitement seeking. The PCL-R in general is related to this, but in particular some elements in Factor 1. Similar to PPI but also includes elements of sub-scales in impulsive antisociality.

I hope with every compassionate bone in my body that none of you have a boss with these qualities. If you are in a relationship with someone with them I would advise you to run for the hills and never look back.

I have two people in my bipolar mind that were separated by 70 years and differing cultures and countries, there would be no match to any DNA or bloodlines whatsoever. However, my contention would be that if we had the ability to cryogenically freeze their minds until man's scientific knowledge of the mind was enlightened it would recognise that they are identical, as if one is being held up to a mirror. What I am clear on is that mental irregularity, unorthodox thinking, can be dangerous and used for wicked acts. It can also make sense of them. I will give you a clue about these 'mind twins.' One was the leader of the most powerful country in the world (with the world's most sadistic hairdresser). The other has as much facial hair above the lip as Charlie Chaplin and a salute like a Roman emperor. No prizes for guessing.

Sadly, you can look back through 2,000 years of history and recognise heads of countries in every part of the globe with these qualities who ruled millions of people. Without a doubt, you can also match religious zealots over time that displayed these qualities, often with the same ruthlessness and brutality. But you won't see this written in your treatment notes or on the consultant's clipboard. Again, I take heart from the words of Winston Churchill: 'If you're going through Hell simply keep going.'

## Meet Kevin my one-time GP

I have known Kevin for many years and he has always maintained (1) that happiness is the best medicine; and (2) you only live once. He is of a time when bedside manner was as important as medical training. He is also the only man I have ever known with a women's shoe fetish, a bona fide eccentric who celebrates his indulgences. Because of these admirable qualities I have always found it easy to talk to him about relationships and matters of the heart.

He has a large and expensive photographic calendar which interestingly only shows one lower leg and foot, the latter in a shoe, always the left leg. He loves going to work each day as he tears off the previous day's shoe to see a new vision of loveliness. He has a way of giving medical facts in a friendly advisory manner making clear the risks within lifestyle choices rather than insulting your intelligence by pointing out the obvious.

At my worst when I was binging on alcohol Kevin would explain the long-term damage in a humorous but honest way saying, 'Frankie the recommended weekly units of alcohol are a maximum and not a target, let alone a licence to consume these in one day's session.' I would concede to his logic then remind him of his annual five-day Test Match benders at Lords cricket ground, or the all-day rugby boys' yard of ale sessions at Twickenham. His reply, 'Ah ... but that's a time-honoured tradition once a year supporting our national teams with my dearest friends. Maybe they do take us slightly over the safe limit, but our nation needs us. It's trip down memory lane which elicits old habits of a time pre-dating the introduction of the said unit recommendations.' Then he would expertly and completely change the subject, remarking, 'What do you think of that dear boy, what a wonderful polka dot kitten heel, simply divine.'

Once I'd been diagnosed with my mental health condition, Kevin would lend perspective to how lucky I was to have modern-day medications and psychiatric support and say that recovery was hard but relatively short in the grand scheme of things.

His father is a wing commander, decorated for his service in the legendary 303 Squadron of Battle of Britain fame. In 42 days his fighter command shot down 126 enemy planes and he held the record of 17 in one mission. His generation served with courage and honour, these servicemen never mentioned how the atrocities they witnessed ravaged their mental health at every battle, every day facing death or watching their friends perish. This living Hell went on for years and the ones that came home suffered the haunting nightmares and vivid flashbacks for decades, still finding the will to recover, to go on, to lead a life. I have the greatest respect and admiration for them and especially for Kevin's dad. He's 83 and recently married his care worker Tiffany who is in her thirties.

The old man is very young at heart, but Kevin's women's shoe fetish is not hereditary. Kevin told me that his father has a lust for life combined with formal military bearing, always in a blazer and tie, with creases in his trousers you could cut a loaf of bread with. He has a full head of grey hair with a precise centre parting. To this day he insists on being called 'Sir' by Kevin — and incidentally by Tiffany. Kevin also loves taking afternoon tea with him, every Sunday, without fail, so as to have a few hours together talking politics or cricket whilst watching Tiffany dust the drawing-room in her French maid's outfit wearing different odd shoes each week, over a pot of Earl Grey and a cucumber sandwich. It's a shame more people are not as dedicated to their elderly parents in the way Kevin is. For me he leads by example.

On a recent visit, the old boy waited till Tiffany was out of earshot, lent forward and said, 'Son, I'm afraid I have a problem ... I don't think I'm enjoying sex anymore?' Kevin coughed-up his Earl Grey, and sent the bone china cup-and-saucer flying high into the air. Fortunately, he is the wicketkeeper for his local cricket club and caught both comfortably shouting, 'Howzat!' His father looked pleased with the catch but perturbed about the problem.

Kevin adopting his bedside manner and reassuring tone said, 'Sir, if I may, at your time of life it is likely to happen, Sir, it does to the best of us, may I ask, Sir, when did you start to notice?' The old boy beamed twiddling his perfectly manicured moustache: 'Twice last night and once this morning.'

I have always respected my elders and try my best to follow their example or at least aspire to it.

## 'A friend of mine has a problem ...'

When I've given guest lectures at colleges and universities, I am always open and honest about my mental health journey, how unwell I was at the time and how I ended up in the system. I'll forever argue the case that I should have gone into hospital, not into prison, but the chaos had to stop. Another of my long suffering GPs called Colin once said the way things were going I would either be sectioned, in prison, or dead. Over time he thankfully only got two out of three right. I mentioned in *Chapter 2* that I was once arrested naked in a stolen kayak. It was clear I was not well. Colin knew it, the police knew it, my solicitor knew it, and when I finally came down from yet another hypermanic episode I definitely knew it.

I always look forward to the Q&A with the students after I've stepped off my soapbox of experience, these Criminology or Social Sciences students are, after all, the future of our criminal justice system. I explain the failing prison system and destructive mental health provision within it. The hardest questions I am asked are in private once the students leave the lecture theatre. I can tell by their posture, their eye-contact, and their voice what they are going to ask. I have spoken to thousands of students over the last seven years or so and, without exception, each of them has a friend or family member who is mentally unwell.

In society, we are moving in the right direction, highlighting and talking about our mental health but this is usually delivered by successful actors, sportsmen and women or musicians, hardly the coal face of serious mental illness and behaviour that destroys ordinary, everyday lives, but nonetheless these celebrities have used their challenges in a positive way which is to be revered. Mental illness is no longer a social taboo, but most people are still very wary of sharing the whole destructive story. I believe there lingers a perceived weakness or fragility in talking openly and honestly. The risk of being labelled 'a nutter' still holds us back.

My 'warts and all' experiences are as disturbing as they are REAL. Students can relate to the carnage, they recognise the same behaviours and episodes and share the experiences of their nearest and dearest and are desperate to help them. In most cases, it gives them the confidence and opportunity to talk openly about issues, behaviours or episodes they have experienced first-hand or next-hand. These are by far the hardest stories to hear and it is impossible to give an answer that will bring comfort, never mind a solution.

I try to explain that there is no one answer, it's not like a physical condition, like diabetes where insulin is the magic bullet. Every person suffering from poor mental health, or a diagnosed condition, is unique. But typically, in a moment of madness, they will not listen to advice, especially from friends or loved ones, and instead pour out or even act out their feelings and erratic thoughts that do not come from a right mind or true self.

If you have a problem you have to admit that you are unwell and that you need professional help, share with family and close friends that you are in a place that is so dark you cannot stand to live like this. At the same time, you're deeply afraid and paranoid of stereotypical images of mental hospitals, padded cells, straightjackets, electric shock treatment and irreversible lobotomies. You fear that if you go into hospital they will never let you out. This is simply the furthest from the truth.

## Where you are is not where you'll be

What cannot be realised until you have journeyed through this experience is that where you are is not where you are going to be. It is a battle to survive, to overcome the darkest of day-to-day trenches of mental illness. You have to:

- tell yourself that you are going into a painful pharmaceutical cocoon that will result in a rebirth;
- resile yourself to losing maybe nine months to a year of your life;
- recognise your mind and body need to rest, you'll maybe sleep for 70 per cent of the time, you will have a poor quality of life; and that
- only your human spirit and your life force can lift you, slowly, day-by-day into a better tomorrow.

At the end of this explanation the students are often in tears and so am I. I feel so much for their plight and know that they are in a position as dire as their loved one.

But at this moment there is always hope and this comes from within, from the human spirit. There is no diagram or sample, but we all know it is real and true. Being able to make sense of my condition has taken years and is a blessing. Talking about the carnage of the past before diagnosis and the journey to recovery is cathartic and allows me to reflect and see how far my recovery has come. With the hardest of work comes the greatest rewards.

The unique abilities in *your* disability will give you strength and wonderful gifts in *your* future. Until you have been at the worst place in life and battled your way back to your best, only then can you truly appreciate the best things in your life and look forwards.

# Chapter 5

## Keep your Heart on the Inside

---

On my first visit to HMP I was in a holding prison with loads of lads from my home town. The boys in here sound like cockneys with a strong local upbringing and mentality. But they have a brilliant sense of humour like Scousers and Brummies. Over hundreds of years the lads back home have defended their territory and fought off everyone, foreign and domestic. Because it's a port there's sailors off the ships looking to visit a few pubs and the local ladies. But the locals won't have them taking liberties with their women and there's often 'skate-bashing'. As one old boy told me, 'They come in the pub looking for a good time and end up in a fight.'

One lad here had been released on licence and within three weeks he was back on the wing, recalled to prison and sporting a fresh tattoo. I approached and asked what happened. He shook his head telling me he'd met his bird, gone out on the lash and got her name tattooed on his arm. A few days later he went to her place to find her in bed with his mate and he ended up battering the guy and she called the police. He had another tattoo on his other arm with another woman's name, so I asked if that was his daughter. He said, 'Nah, it's my last bird … she gave me the sack and ended up with my cousin.'

We were with the wing cleaner who cracked up recommending that the guy should stay away from tattoo parlours in future before he ran out of skin. The lad with the tattoo then told us another tale about a romance he'd had years back. I'm pleased to share it with you.

## Blind date

'I fell in love once, never again, her name was Gina, she knocked me off my feet. I found her on a dating website, her profile said she was a pound in front, a virgin, and lived in my neck of the woods.

She asked me to meet her in *The Mystery*, not so much a gastro pub, more a spit and sawdust juicer. It had some quaint touches. The tables, chairs and beer mats were all nailed down and the welcome from the regulars was straight out of *The Slaughtered Lamb* in "American Werewolf in London." Interestingly everyone was smoking in there, and as I ordered my pint I said "Mush it's illegal to smoke in pubs." The barman replied, "The gavvers* are all barred."

I looked around but couldn't seem to match her profile picture to any of the birds, I hoped she might have just gone for an eye lash. Then this voice shouts out from the corner table surrounded by smoke, and I could make out the silhouette of a bouncer. So, I swaggers over as the smoke lifts, she looks like Harry Redknapp in a wig, a mush with a bush. I reckoned it must be Shelley's mate. I sit down get my bag of sniff out and rack up a line.

"Where's Shelley?" She leaned forward snatched my rolled-up score off me, hovered up my livener and put the score in her sweaty cleavage. She challenged me to try and retrieve my dough, but I didn't fancy my chances, no point being a squinney,† so I chopped another and had a quick blast.

"Shelley had to nip back to the bedsit, her old man is kicking-off, he found her phone and saw she was on the dating website. He's gonna get a few dry slaps and rag-dolled about it, proper fool he is." She laughed and slapped me on the back as I was lighting my blower. I torched my nostrils and broke it in two.

"Christ's sake Divi behave yourself," I screeched. I recognised her from

---

\*    Police.

†    Someone who moans or complains.

somewhere, but wasn't sure where. She told me to get her a shant* and a packet of scampi fries. I'd just been weighed in from a bit of graft and I was flush so went to the bar and shouted the mush over when he whispered, "Mate, I would leave that bird well alone if I was you." I thought, "Who's this numpty?" so I paid him with a moody score, he didn't even twig.

I passed her the pint and the fries, it was a touch 'cause her breath was well mangy. She ate the bag in one mouthful, didn't even take them out of the packet!

"What's your name love? ... You're some sort of nutter aren't you, you know my brothers."

The penny dropped.

"Sod it, sure I does, mush we were nicking a few quid last year but my supplier is banged up."

I could now see the family resemblance, she looked like her brothers. She was the moneylender of the firm, I'd never had any favours off her lot so always had a giggle with them. Still, I didn't want to get involved so necked my beer and stood-up to leave but she was having none of it. She put her arm on my shoulder and dragged me back to my chair like a sack of spuds. I tried to blag her I had to go see a man about a dog but she put her fat, nicotine-stained fingers over my lips.

"Sshhh lover boy you came for a jump and I've got the right horn."

I tried to spin out of her grasp and jump-up, but she moved like lightning. Her left hand grabbed my cobblers, the other was around my throat. Her half sovereigns and keeper rings on each finger were crushing my windpipe, I couldn't move, I was snookered. She pulled me close and whispered, "Let's not play games, the minute you walked in I knew we were going to be together. I always know if my flaps flutter and in those Armani jeans ... Wheee ... you got an arse like a 12-year-old boy."

---

\* Drink.

If I couldn't match her for strength maybe I could talk my way out of it.

"Listen love my Mum's expecting me home for my tea, I'll come straight back in a few hours, trust me I have never let you lot down."

No joy, she kept her vice like grip, she looked me in the eye and said with a big grin, "Fight me or have me."

I was powerless to her charms and strength. She necked her pint, stood-up, grabbed her moody Louis Vuitton bag and put the pint glasses into it. I could see into her bag and went white as a sheet when I noticed a pack of cable ties, a bottle of poppers and a strap on dildo. She then lovingly lifted me over her shoulder and walked me back to my shitbox.

Some of the boys were coming toward us but quickly crossed over when they recognised her mooey. I was that desperate I tried to phone the gavvers, but as I got my phone out of my pocket it slipped and hit the deck. It couldn't get any worse as that was my graft phone, so I was losing a few quid as well. Wounded. As she forced me to open the door she grabbed me again, pushed me up against the wall, and the rising damp soaked my face as she growled, "How do you want your toffee apple? Teeth in or teeth out?"

That was a night I'll never forget. I can close my eyes 15 years on and tremble. I feel my stomach churn, my cobblers tense up trying to ingest into my body, and tears start to well-up in my eyes. I often wake up in the night, with intense and vivid dreams of her. I jump up and run to the window looking for her huge silhouette, but she's not there. I'll never forget her words after 72 hours as she cut the cable ties (that she called friendship bracelets).

"If you love them set them free, if they come back its true love."

I still know little about what women want from a geezer, I used to think that fat birds were like mopeds, great fun to ride until your mates see you on one... but not anymore. I'm still game so who knows what'll happen next, I've learned two things though. Stay away from dating websites with the word "pro" in the title and sit with your back to the wall in *The Mystery.*'

## Two sides to every relationship

Everyone's relationship is unique and the only people who really know the whole story are the two people involved. From personal experience and the stories of others, break-ups rarely end well, they just end. There are two sides to every story and so at least two versions about why a relationship failed. These then multiply into biased versions from the friends of each party. Then they mutate into fiction from the friends of friends who don't even know the two people involved. They become *Jackanory* stories.

I think relationship courses should be discreetly offered for those HMP guests released on licence and at risk of being recalled, e.g. due to a 'non-violent but heated and loud domestic argument.' I was shocked at the number of prisoners who told their version of events where the neighbours called the police, they came, and the protocol was to remove the prisoner. Now, defusing the situation I completely understand but it does seem there can be a lack of equality in establishing who is the antagonist and who the victim.

One of my pad mates from my first sentence let his ex-girlfriend into his house and once inside she called the police and said she'd been kidnapped. They attended and even though the woman didn't live there they followed the protocol leading to his recall to prison. A week or so later he spoke to his solicitor who said the girlfriend had dropped the charges and admitted she'd not been kidnapped at all. The prisoner in this case was the victim and still had to serve the rest of his sentence in custody as he was back in the system.

I know that people need to be properly protected but the prisoner term for this kind of situation is 'wounded.' It's laugh or cry and we laugh because it is funny, and we laugh because it's the tragic truth. The following day that pad mate had the last laugh though when a big fat envelope arrived for me from my own wife, it was my divorce papers. Always nice to get post and my pad mate had hours of fun reading all the reasons for her petition.

I was also 'wounded' as these were one version of my behaviour whilst I was mentally unwell and in episodes. but they were all true versions and still my responsibility, although without malice or guilty purpose. To borrow a legal phrase there was no *mens rea*. Yet sat in the cell that night it felt like I was being shafted again by my soon to be ex-ball and chain's lawyers. Till death us do part can translate into 'until they really harm or even kill each other' if the red mist descends into a crime of passion.

## On the bright side

Tonight I spoke to my new Lucky Lady. She was on good form, but the phone credit went way too fast. 'Bless her,' I thought, she'd sent three letters to my local remand prison, so I explained the detour and gave her my new address. Without doubt, in my heart this was the hardest part of my HMP experience this time around (alongside talking to my children), something I didn't have on my last visit. Back then my life was in freefall, and I'd no idea what the future would look like. But although I now knew I'd soon be free of my marriage and hoped to be with someone new, would I be able to stop future episodes?

This time I'd met someone very special, and we'd been apart since lockdown so three months was now turning into at least two-and-half more until I was released. I thought, 'You want to hear her voice but then you run out of credit and you sit in your flowery dell and the heartache hits you like an express train.'

What I couldn't do was let her know the sadness I was feeling but I did want her to know that I missed her so much I couldn't bear it, more than I would ever have thought possible. Prison is an emotional sentence, you just have to ride-out, but it is ten times harder than the physical punishment of being behind bars.

I take heart from knowing I'm very lucky as I trust Lucky Lady completely, and that I've never met anyone quite like her before. I also delude myself that she's punching above her weight, but we have both loved and lost, so we know who we are and what we want, we just have to wait for each other. In my heart, knowing someone is there for me is powerful and gives me inner strength when I need it most, a connection that travels over the walls and takes me to her, and her to me. I'm an incurable romantic and love potion is potent.

## And on the not so bright side …

Some prisoners end relationships as they can't handle the physical sentence let alone the emotional one, which tears some of them apart, it's just too mentally destructive. Over longer sentences, they can detach completely. If the relationship is volatile, because love can drive you to insanity, or simple incompatibility, and trust is fragile, the paranoia of what is happening outside while you are inside brings more torture. Often this perfect storm can lead to complete emotional shutdown, making prisoners devoid of feelings altogether, devoid of empathy, and this affects their mental health.

More and more prisoners are getting to the end of their rope, and the healthcare beds are reserved only for the growing failed suicide bid squad. What is surreal is the emotional sentence on the other side of the wall. I remember a gay prisoner telling me his fella at home was paranoid and giving him loads of grief on the phone by suggesting that the prisoner was going to meet another guy in prison. The conversation got heated and the prisoner shouted down the phone, 'I've met eight hundred fellas on my wing, and I'm living with two at the minute due to overcrowding!'

## Is there a secret to relationships?

When lockdown first started, I sent Lucky Lady a copy of *The Alchemist* by the Brazilian author Paulo Coelho, just as soon as I'd read it. When she received it, she devoured the whole thing in one sitting but a couple of lines took her breath away:

> 'She would have to send her kisses on the wind, hoping that the wind would touch the boy's face, and would tell him that she was alive … in that moment the Earth turned to bring us closer, it turned on itself and on us until it finally brought us together.'

South Americans are known for their passion and there is nothing quite like a Brazilian to get the blood pumping.

Who knows the secret to a healthy and happy relationship? Forget separate bathrooms, maybe separate houses? Could personal hygiene and trimmed pubic hair or not having kids or pets be another key ingredient? A work-life balance, or not living beyond your means, enjoying your jobs and having at least two holidays a year. To my mind, there are lots of stresses but I believe there are four crucial ingredients:

- Equal attraction and a meeting of minds so as to want and need intimacy from one another.
- The courage to be completely honest with each other.
- Biting your tongue till you bleed to death.
- The ability to make each other laugh and to share laughter together.

These I think are the most important things in life, they nurture us, fulfil us, keep us mentally strong. We feel more relaxed, more alive, we have a lust for life, are young at heart, a twinkle in our eye.

## 'Anger'

Martin (aka 'Anger') *always* had a twinkle in *his* eye and I was completely shocked at the news his heart had given out. I couldn't and wouldn't believe it. We often compared notes on which of us was the most mentally unwell, or the carnage we'd created. It was 'honours even' I think, a closely fought contest, a draw. He was also bipolar and like me came from a background where men's feelings were rarely expressed. This apart, he could talk for England (and most other countries including his native Scotland). He had a brain the size of a planet, the heart of a lion, memory of an elephant, more mischief than the Norse God Loki, and a life force and spirit that healed troubled minds and opened hearts. Mental illness made the pair of us the blackest of sheep in our families, but Anger could take the weight from my shoulders.

I remember the condolence messages. From his landlord — 'Dear Anger. You have one week to clear your shit out, even though you're paid up for three, I don't believe the rumour you've died, pull the other one. Three weeks is to cover the cost of the missing copper pipe and radiators. Don't ever try renting from me again.' The boys at the scrapyard — 'Gutted … the boss is asking what the Pearly Gates are made of and how much they weigh?' The Car Crime Unit — 'We'd like to thank you for leaving this Earth, owners of XR3is, Cosworths and GTEs can sleep easier. Please contact the police station and let the gaoler know where to send your slippers'. Your No1 Governor, HMP — 'It's come to notice you owe £4.24 in phone credit. Being dead is a poor excuse according to the Ministry of Justice. They may be forced to recall your ashes to the seg.'

Anger wasn't perfect, never pretended to be, and anyone who heard him singing his heart out knew just how well (and like me) he could murder a tune. Yet as a fellow gambler on life he made me feel brave enough to be honest with myself.

## The best bipolar things in life are free

I always knew 'the best things in life were free.' Even when I didn't have them. I kept the faith and never gave up looking. Now I have finally found those things I know it's definitely true. I keep the faith and try to think of it not as a cliché, rather doctor's orders, so as to be happy and live life to the full.

We are like any species on the planet—driven by procreation in order for the human race to survive. The physical act is the easy bit to understand. The mind's connection with the act itself is much more fun to think about, our deep-rooted knowledge through education is equally warped for both sexes. To paraphrase the *Bible*: 'It was the disobedience of Adam and Eve, who'd been told by God not to eat of the tree (Genesis 2:17), that caused disorder in creation, thus humanity inherited sin and guilt from their sin.' Nice to get the view of the church on matters of the heart. An apple a day only keeps the doctor away it would appear.

## Man (or woman) with two brains syndrome

I think I speak for many men when I say we can all be sinful, suffer from 'man with two brains syndrome.' It is really two minds, the first of which is caring and the second perverse and located between the legs. I've witnessed the perversion of married men with respectable jobs whose actions are quite different. Women are also capable of this I think, but that's another bipolar story. In my manic mind I'm convinced that the secret lives of both sexes must use equal parts of both types of brain yet with discipline and practice we can create alchemy. Sinful behaviour can be unleashed daily at no cost and the merest suggestion of eye-contact or hip gyration. What's it worth? Easy ... It's priceless.

# Chapter 6

The First Ice Age of the Human Spirit

When I was a kid we lived in a simpler time and place where we did what we were told. We respected our parents implicitly, and you never answered back, or you got a smack. We never asked our parents for money or gifts unless it was our birthday or Christmas and the Mummy or Daddy taxi service had not been invented. You had legs and you used them. We were lucky enough to have food in our bellies, shoes on our feet and possessions were handed down and looked after. I was a happy soul with a carefree spirit which I am pleased to say has returned to me all these years later. I am what I once was.

## Colour television

What we did have was a TV and it was colour, but it was switched-off more than switched-on, so there was no danger of getting square eyes or overexposure to radio waves. It was only watched in the evenings apart from bath night when you could watch the Sunday afternoon Western and the darts. I used to love 'Star Trek.' It first appeared on the gogglebox one Wednesday at 6 pm. You rarely found out what was on the telly beforehand, so it was the best surprise on the planet. I watched it once and was hooked. There were lots of reasons for this, including that the character in charge, Captain T J Hooker (William Shatner) liked to pull a bird no matter from which species or how far-flung from Planet Earth. His mission was always to seek out new life, get some strange alien girlfriend and take his craft to warped speeds, even when an engineer was recommending in a Scottish accent, 'She can't take the power captain.'

## 'Beam me up Scotty'

It was not all about being perverse in the Universe. I also liked the adventure and the knowledge that there were not just humans in the stratosphere but pointy-eared fellas who could knock you out by squeezing your collar bone, and beautiful telephonists with mini-skirts who were skilled in linguistics and had the reddest lips and best features. I'd never met a black woman in the flesh but wanted to, very much.

I beamed aboard *The Enterprise* every week through the unpaid TV licence and went into space, the final frontier, my mission the same as Jim Kirk and his crew, meaning to seek out new life, to go where no man had gone before. I'd been doing a version of this in real life anyway taking every opportunity to go meet the world, one adventure at a time. I didn't have a spaceship, a phaser gun, or a teleport but in my imagination the spirit of adventure beamed me and my fertile mind to a real place and real people that I came across.

I also loved superheroes. They were a bit thin on the ground back then, mainly Superman and Spiderman. I thought they were quite believable, but I never wanted to be one or have special powers, I've no idea why. We also had Adam West as Batman the caped crusader—fighting crime and baddies that were up to no good nicking money from banks, making weapons or lusting for power, with plans for mind control over everyone in Gotham City. Repeats of the camp 1960s version, not the dark, brooding, serious-minded incarnation of Batman in today's blockbuster movies. Batman's sidekick Robin was surplus to requirements but to me his butler Alfred was cool as could be. So was the Batphone, secret panels, the fireman's pole to the Bat Cave, and the Batmobile, Batbike and Batboat (none of which Robin got to drive ever!). I wasn't interested in putting my undercrackers on over my tracksuit bottoms or wearing a mask and running around with unusually slow arm movements that were not the coolest to watch. In fact, thinking back now it's odds-on that Batman and Robin either both had severe piles or were pretty affectionate toward each other. After all, they did come from wealthy and privileged backgrounds. Old Alfred must have seen some sights, maybe on occasion taking one for the team.

Neither did I want to be any of the villains. The only power I would have gone out of my way to obtain was the Joker's capacity for laughter. Mate, he loved a giggle but maybe that was because he could laugh at the absurdity of the world being portrayed.

Superhero TV shows were out there, like a box set, but TV only showed them one at a time, so you had to wait a whole week to see the next adventure. Waiting a week is not a big deal, honest it really isn't, try it! You'll see then if you have the discipline. Please be aware that binging media content is as addictive as any other toxin. I would use stories and stimuli to add to my mental adventures and before I knew it a week had gone by. Steve Austin was 'The Million Dollar Man' and had some bionic upgrades, pulling a few stunts against the baddies and telling us all a very important lesson for life, which I am not sharing with you. Please get your own.

### Wonder Woman and the A-Team

What I'll never, ever forget as an early coming-of-age eleven-year-old was the best creature on the planet. Wonder Woman had superhuman strength and speed, breasts that defied gravity and a hold-up metal bra, full glossy red lips and the ability to tie up baddies with a whip or rope, which made them tell the truth, the lucky so and so's.

Linda Evans the actress who played Wonder Woman was sadly the victim of rumours that she was an ex-soft porn star just because she'd been a glamour model. Fake news I guess, but I put my hands up to not only hearing this blatant gossip but spreading it far and wide. Wonder Woman took me to Fantasy Land loads of times in different locations usually with my trousers around my ankles. Unlike Supergran who was on daytime telly for the kids but I'm not going to go through that one — it's enough to say the best thing was the theme tune. 'She makes them look like a bunch of fairies, got more bottle than United Dairies.' Supergran had fighting spirit, and a tartan hat and handbag.

And I 'don't want to cause a ruckus for B A Baracus.' The A-Team were on the run from the authorities (they'd escaped from a maximum security prison) helping local communities, being paid in cabbages or shirt buttons. I think deep down they would have done it for nothing, or the cost of the millions of rounds of ammunition that were fired at baddies each week never hitting the target.

You also had some interesting anti-heroes to feed your imagination. A scientist who used too much Gamma Ray in the lab and was now on the run as he tried to find the cure. His tagline could be used by absolutely anybody, anywhere and at any time in history except perhaps Mahatma Ghandi: 'Don't make me angry, you won't like me when I'm angry.' He travelled light as he didn't make it through one episode without ripping his clobber.

## Comic capers

I didn't really do comics until later in life, I used to read *Viz* religiously but that was in my mid-20s, feeding my warped sense of humour. I did do *2000 AD* for a while and had a big poster of Slaine on my wall, He was a cool-looking guy with a battle axe, an eye patch and a goblin for a sidekick.

I also loved Asterix who it was awesome to read about, even though it was a French story. He was fearless and fought for justice. Asterix's society was under threat, had been invaded and their rights violated. I had some *Asterix* annuals (think box set for weekly comics), in which they fought the Roman Empire. They had great community spirit. There's nothing more ferocious than human beings defending their homes, families and way of life.

Asterix had several things going for him. He didn't look French, he had a winged helmet, he had a cool little Jack Russell, and a massive best mate called Obelix and they were in combat with an enemy with no fighting spirit, even though it had far superior weaponry and numbers. They knew a druid who made a potion that the community took together (including the Jack Russell) before battle, which was a tribal ritual. MATE … they were off the chart, on a whole different level, smashing the life out of Romans, with shields and helmets flying everywhere and having a giggle during the battle with their mates, big smiles, team-tagging their victims, the Jack Russell acting like Bruce Lee with its one-inch paw kicks. The saying, 'It is not the size of the dog but the size of the heart that beats inside it' reads true in this regard.

Once they'd twatted their opponents they would neatly pile up the bodies, write 'Romans Go Home' on the chest of the solitary soldier still standing and release him back to the Roman Commander (who had less fighting spirit after witnessing the druid juice fuelled enemy). The winners would go back to camp for a knees-up and some more druid juice as it didn't make them psychotic it just made them supreme. Like snooker champion Alex 'Hurricane'

Higgins on 15 pints of Guinness. The ingredients for each may be different but deliver the same pure genius within their own discipline.

### Monkey Magic

Monkey Magic was a free spirit and will always be one of my most joyful experiences as a child on my own. The programme was fantastic, like nothing I'd ever seen before. Later in life whilst locked away with nothing to do I read the book. The story is 3,000 years old but the message more ancient. Those that please themselves, lie, steal binge on toxins or food, and ignore the rules have loads more fun than the rest of us.

I was educated to the knowledge that there are such things as evil monsters and spirits. They take many forms and have to be faced up to and beaten, usually by a collection of people, not just one individual. The priest who Monkey protected explained that there is no such thing as an evil person, only evil or misguided acts that deliver an evil end result. We all have the ability to do good deeds or misguided ones.

The moral of this familiar story seems to be that you can live like a king, steal and swindle all the wealth in the world but you will sit alone on your throne and die of sadness and loneliness without love and faith in yourself. If you do good and help as many people as you can, even when you feel least able, by doing an act of kindness, it will not leave you cold or hungry or in harm's way. You will never be empty inside and you will never be afraid. I was 100 per cent sold on this but what I wouldn't give to get a cloud you can summon by passing your fingers over your lips whilst blowing, and a magic staff that can be as small as a matchstick or as big as a telegraph pole. Then you *have* made it in the world.

## Turning into my own Mum

No matter what medium is used to transfer knowledge the outcome is learning more about the world and forces within it. These stories were a tiny fraction of the adventures and influences I came across growing-up in very different environments with lots and lots of different new people. I would say that back then people's sense of community spirit was far stronger than what I see today, because more people made the effort to talk directly to each other. They went out of their way to do that. It is clear to me that learning about the human spirit is at its most potent through human contact, seeing and hearing and feeling with your own senses, and watching the individual spirits become the collective community spirit.

We all have the same inevitable journey of growing older and more responsible. It seems that our spirit fades or is neglected in the mundane trenches of everyday life. We use the phrase, 'Kids today they don't know they're born' once we have children, as we fail to comprehend why they think they can do what they want, when they want, each and every day.

There are modes of parenting that I've seen with my own eyes. Giving children every treat that they ask for and bending to their will each time, because parents love their offspring so much, or because they were given nothing at their children's ages. Because their parents couldn't afford it and they can. We fail to grasp that a child can't expect constant rewards without doing something to deserve them, which has to stem from the parents. It is often as likely that some parents feel guilty and ashamed because they have *less* than their parents did and can barely afford the bills let alone a treat. When I say, 'Kids today, they don't know they're born' my whole body instantly shudders. I picture my Mum saying it to me. Aaarrrgghhhh, could I be turning into my parents? Don't panic we're not becoming *our* parents we have simply become parents and now have the mammoth task of navigating how to bring up our children, how to deal with the eternal question of what makes good parenting. Even when you know inside, instinctively, what is best and what is right you will still feel at times that you betray yourself to please your children, it's not been labelled 'the hardest job in the world' for nothing.

Our lack of community spirit is growing and reflects individual ignorance of our personal human spiritual development, also of a huge responsibility as we get older. We can blame technology for the lack of community connection, although it has the ability to connect us in new ways which should be a huge advantage over past generations.

We can blame our lack of discipline as parents or claim that the single parent family or separation of parents is far greater than in the past. We can blame the teachers and the schools for putting admin before inspiring their pupils and being role models. We can blame modern society that prescribes what can and can't be said, putting political correctness way, way above common sense. It is the collective responsibility of all of us to put our hands up together and each take some of the blame and ask, 'How do we get better?'

## Building a moral compass

To learn how to improve in our human and community spirit we are perhaps best served by looking at past values. Freedom was a blessing for kids, you were allowed to walk the streets of your home town (or village) including to school on your own from as young as eight-years-old. You were simply warned about talking to strangers or accepting gifts if they were offered. I am fortunate to say that I had a very happy spirit growing-up in places with a healthy community spirit which shaped my early socialisation and built my moral compass and ethics, the standards I wanted to live by or aspired to emulate. You may not feel that this type of learning suits you, you need something with more structure to give you faith.

There are stories that build loads of useful things for the future, but I think the ones people hold dearest are the ones that feed the human spirit. This is best achieved when you are younger as that I believe is when you are most connected with them. I was lucky in this realisation through the programmes I watched, it came to me earlier in life, which always helps, like learning a language or becoming a sports prodigy. Without mind, body, spirit we can never reach our true potential in human connection and growth. As with an athlete this needs consistent training and discipline.

I learned this through other TV programmes, which we were lucky to have when growing-up. 'Highway to Heaven' was a wonderful show, full of my favourite things, a nomadic existence, helping people who are in trouble, and breathing life into lost souls. The heroic duo were one part human and the other part supernatural, guardian angels, but both needing each other to teach people that within themselves lies the answer to their problems. The same ingredients were used in 'The Littlest Hobo' but this time the hero was a scruffy mongrel dog that had more communication skills than Lassie and Flipper put together and a theme tune that captivated me. The words made me dream of the world being my home, making friends, traveling light, moving on and never settling down.

When you are conceived you are made up 100 per cent of human spirit from the unity of a man and a woman in the rare state of orgasm, plus there are fluids and all the other anatomical stuff. Created with the same fire that lit the stars and the Cosmos. Hence the orgasm is mind-blowing, mystical, heavenly, beautiful, quivering, or if you're lucky an out-of-body experience, where you're literally sent to Heaven and back seeing stars. Forgive the pun but this is a repeat of the BIG Bang theory. Regardless of the level of orgasm achieved during the sexual act it is still a spiritual and metaphysical 'coming together.'

A guide has been placed before us to help us on our spiritual journey. An ancient principle before religion prescribed a way of life for us to follow. Its symbol, an eye framed in a triangle, the all-seeing eye, set down across cultures and continents in stone, in wood and on papyrus. Its principles have always been needed, they involve tolerance and respect for all living things and the opinions of all people. It asks us to behave with kindness and understanding, to practise charity and to care for our community and to volunteer our time to help others. It holds the truth at its centre and in our actions which makes us moral to ourselves and each other. These are the keys to the joy of life, happiness, and of the world we inhabit.

## Like living in a Gothic novel

So how have we evolved into neglecting the truth and choosing rules and penalties that make our lives so much less joyful and are destructive to our world? Why are they enforced by the powerful rulers of cultures that clearly break communities whilst keeping the ancient principles intact for themselves? It is as if we are living today in a perpetual Gothic novel, where we are supposed to follow the supposed decency of civilised and respectable society but by indulging the depravity and debauchery and then lying about it to the world and ourselves. We can all see that these devices are immoral and destructive and yet we follow them. It feels as if the only explanation is that our metaphysical selves have been invaded or controlled by a spirit that is alien to us. We are now told stories that deceive us and point us to the wrong path. Without the truth of the human spirit, we are led by them for guilty purposes. It is the 'heroin of the mind' and we are all guilty of being either users or addicts. Only the rare few are immune to it. I wish I was one of them. I would like to meet one some day.

In the modern world it seems we've been deceived and controlled over time to where we are now by something that seeks to harm us. In the UK we are I believe without doubt the most subservient and obedient country in Europe, we should be deeply ashamed of ourselves. A nanny state that has let down Sir Captain Tom's generation and all those who fought to protect us, but also our children who will be in the hands of the total control of 'the computer [that] says no.' Unless we make the right and proper decision to bring these ancient principles back and lead our lives by them. Now!

Maybe that's why the human spirit has been given the COVID pandemic as a lesson to our species that our way of life will destroy ourselves and our world. I can believe that this is Mother Nature's way of thinning the herd as it has done throughout history. There is nothing new in this. But in the modern world of mind control and influence the path is far more dangerous than during the plagues and infections of the past.

This time the powerful cannot protect themselves and they do not have the answers to spoon feed the masses. The confusion it causes in the basic logic of cause and effect is not only lost but contradicted in a way that causes more harm and greater spread of infection. For months families saw lonely and painful deaths of loved ones taken into hospital (or were prevented from seeing them). The truth is that life is precious and fragile.

People are being forced by nature to re-evaluate what is the most important thing in life, each other, and consider that the human spirit is desperately needed for us to survive. We have all the medication we need but not the balance, we are a force of human nature eating itself away, leaving a shell.

## Rats in a pellet feeder

COVID has revealed the best in some people's human kindness and the worst in others by showing their true colours and sometimes hollow characters. Those that are destructive and selfish are so blinded by fear that illogical beliefs from uneducated and unqualified sources are seen as truth. To believe that COVID is a conspiracy, or it has been man-made to harm others is insanity. This is of our own making, but it feeds the horror.

We have created a dystopia by neglecting our human spirit and near total mind control of how to think and what to think about. Our thoughts are prescribed and values that are harmful to themselves. We are under-educated and over-medicated, the grooming process. We are not required to be given tangible explanations, no real reason to comply, nor receive a return on investment spiritually, or societally. We are becoming masses who are like blind lab rats trapped in a pellet feeder.

The ancient principles need to be reborn in us all: everyone in the world needs to recognise that we are on this planet to help each other. Selfless not selfish, the truth, not lies, the evil of profit and power has manufactured consent which never benefits the masses who deliver it. Wherever we are in the world in any given time in our brief lifespans is exactly where we are supposed to be. Ever heard the phrase 'right place at the right time'—it works both ways—'wrong place at the wrong time'—which makes me believe we are heading towards being helpless twigs in the waters of a mighty stream.

In some 200 years of successive generations, we have become collectively responsible for destroying our planet and the legacy of debt and financial hardship on the horizon. Our children's children will see that we have made their future lives so much harder than they should ever have been. We have neglected the ancient principles, and we now have to reap what we sowed. COVID will not decimate children in the same way it will the old as somehow it knows kids are not to blame, so they will not suffer the wrath.

I have lived a life and if I have to perish so that my own children can survive in a world where the human spirit is returned to its rightful place as the most precious of possessions then it will be a sacrifice well made. We are in the First Ice Age of the Human Spirit.

## Amulets and muscle memory

But do not despair. The world will keep spinning and those of us who still have a strong human spirit will survive, an amulet for protection. You can also dig deep and reconnect with your spirit, like muscle memory it was always 100 per cent us when we were conceived, and it still is I promise you.

It is easier to believe if you are abnormal or have mental health challenges, you can only learn if you suspend your rational spoon-fed mind-controlled heroin-like haze. It's never too late. We still have time to 'just say no' and save ourselves. Being crazy really is an asset for this new spiritual future, not a disability, have faith in the truth of that.

# Chapter 7

Another Day in Paradise Lost

Liverpool are the COVID Premier League champions after beating Crystal Palace to take a 23-point lead that no-one can catch. Shock, horror, like this sentence, I never saw that coming. A shame for the fans that it's been a 30-year wait. That's a stretch I don't think I could ever manage behind bars.

'Sign on, sign on with hope in your heart 'cause you'll never get a job, you'll never get a job, sign on, sign on.'

This is sometimes sung by away supporters at Liverpool's ground, Anfield, in an attempt to drown out the home supporters singing 'Walk on, walk on, with hope in your heart.' Five thousand of us visiting fans sang our version when we drew them in the Carling Cup. It was really 800 true away supporters and 4,200 locals who fancied a day out and the chance to take the mickey out of the Red shite as my Dad would call them. As I said at the start of this book, he's an Evertonian. One year we got him a T-shirt which said 'One Evertonian is worth Ten Liverpudlians.' Is that right Dad?

### Sweet memories

I'm starting to realise that I'm again a prisoner, it's not a pleasant feeling, but what this clearly illustrates is that you can never build a prison for my bipolar brain. My day has started with sweet memories of a proper day out with all the top boys and my big bro, and we were drawing 2-2 at half time and singing our arses off.

'Who nicked my stereo. You nicked my stereo. Who nicked my stereo? You nicked my stereo.'

We kept Liverpool's Kop quiet for the first 45 minutes, 5,000 voices from a third of a stand versus 40,000 (not all their season ticket holders came as we're a lower league side) surrounding us as some of the most passionate and vocal supporters of any club in the world. The fairytale didn't last too long as in the second 45 minutes they scored three, but my voice was like 'sea biscuit' — a little ho(a)rse. I was gutted that they televised another game — a 0-0 thriller. *C'est la vie.*

### Noise, noise, and even more noise

In my HMP Hotel there's a clear regime and rules for us inmates. Then there are those that bend the rules, seasoned prisoners, men of will and you can spot them a mile away. All HMP Hotels share a constant soundtrack: keys jangling, men shouting, enclosed inmates smashing cell doors. This turns your stomach and violates your senses, it causes anxiety to every prisoner at the start of their sentence no matter how many times they've been inside. It's a human reaction when in an oppressive, inhumane environment and I can tell you that for a first-time offender it takes far more to adjust to than anything else. Their anxiety is visible when they are out of their cell on the wing. The trick is to get used to it as soon as possible before this visible anxiety causes you to fall victim to seasoned inmates.

Opened-up by the governor for meds and on my slow amble up the wing, I pick up a copy of the freebie prison newspaper *Inside Time*, a publication that's been the voice of prisoners since the late-1970s. It's the only red top I'd ever recommend, headed up by Erwin James an ex-offender who became a published writer and *Guardian* journalist and it is edited by Noel 'Razor' Smith. Noel was a 'professional' bank robber who spent 32 years behind the door then became a journalist and writer, with several books for Penguin (now Penguin Random House one of the biggest publishing houses in the world). I had the privilege of meeting Erwin who wrote an article about my *Little Book of Prison: A Beginner's Guide* in the *Guardian*, and I later met him at *Inside Time's* head office. I'm looking forward to reading that newspaper.

In my humble opinion there's a balancing act to socialising with fellow inmates. I wouldn't recommend being a 'social leper' inside but don't be too eager to make new friends either. Be sociable with everyone, common courtesy and eye-contact (but not for too long), nod to acknowledge anyone you pass or that passes you, and be aware of whoever is behind you, at all times, not just in the showers!

What I do know this second time around is that my sentence will be served in my mind. To have a positive mindset is crucial. Very difficult at the beginning but a necessity. I am lucky to understand a growth mindset, I choose to face and overcome challenges, it's taken half-a-century but it is now my mantra. Where you are in this world is not where you are going to be.

My menu sheet has slid through the crack in the door from 'The Hustler.' He opens the flap (a slither of glass you can look through) and shouts me over from my desk. He gets the screw to open the door and hands me a pouch of coffee and some vape capsules. RESULT! The door closes but he stays there, he slides a piece of paper with a prisoner's name and number on it for me to make the payment to. I give my thanks and ask him for the man's details and say I'll send him a drink. He declines but it always pays to offer. I tell him what a cushy number he has for a job, he's the laundry man. NICE one. 'No wonder your clobber looks fresh.'

He asks if I want the flap left open or closed, another courtesy as most prisoners want it to be left open so they can watch for a passing worker to run an errand or two. I respond by saying 'Closed, I'm trying to get some work done.' He shuts it, and off he goes leaving me to put the kettle on and celebrate with a strong coffee and a fresh vape capsule. Happy days.

The trade has also got me the menu sheet far earlier than I would usually get it so I can pick all the protein foods to feed the muscles after the cell workouts and avoid cheese on the Chef's Special as I detest it, mouldy milk the Devil's work. Another sweet if small victory.

## Worse than the Chef's Special

I can tell you that you can't put a price on freedom, you only work that out when you are denied it on an hourly, daily, weekly, monthly and yearly basis (fortunately I've not had this last experience). No matter what you made in profits if you were a real career criminal the lack of freedom is always too big a price to pay. The taxpayer can put a price on it as holding a prisoner costs society in the region of £60,000 per year. Times that by 90,000 and think about how much of this monster sum is spent on rehabilitation. Not a lot. UK re-offending rates are the highest in Europe because of this lack of investment.

All previous Governments, red or blue, Boris or Blair, have held the same position of 'prevention not cure' because it's a solid message for vote-winning purposes in the run-up to an election. Tough on crime is adopted by each and every political party, maybe not in Europe, just in our green and pleasant land. As Winston Churchill once said, 'The mood and the temper of the public in regard to the treatment of crime and criminals is one of THE MOST unfailing tests of the civilisation of any country' (my own emphasis). Mind you Churchill was probably three sheets to the wind when he said this, he did have a rare ability to consume vast quantities of alcohol regardless of whose company he was in and especially when working. In defence of his intake, he did say, 'I took more from drink than drink ever took out of me' and he was a prisoner of war. One of his favourite tipples was whisky 'the water of life.' We have all seen people who are at the mercy of the bottle, and when the bottle reaches their lips it sucks the life out of them. I beg everyone to consider and acknowledge that there is a huge difference between excess and addiction, in my excessively bipolar opinion.

The modern political position and the blatant lack of responsibility for a more civil and inclusive society is something I find even more difficult to stomach than my Chef's Special.

### Don't believe everything you hear in prison

No matter which prison you are unlucky enough to be in you will hear it said that the jail you are in is *the worst there is*. Difficult to believe this as there are around 120 prisons in the UK and thousands and thousands around the globe. Also that Category A prisons alongside young offender institutions (YOIs) have 30 per cent more violence than the Cat B hotel I'm in. You hear it from the lips of most prisoners, but as I stated in my five golden rules in my *Little Book of Prison,* 'Don't believe everything you hear in HMP.'

Another valuable pastime during my first few days is signing-up for everything possible. Alcohol Abuse Support, Drug Abuse Support, Anger Management, Being a Buddhist, anything to get the cell door open. My medication guarantees at least one stroll down the wing per day. I'm lucky to be crazy, but no-one would notice that in prison anyway. I will defo check the books next time I'm out, what brilliant works of literature will there be? What masterpiece awaits to transcend these walls in my mind.

I consider myself lucky to have planned my 'going to prison bag.' I have A4 pads, pencils, a rubber and pencil sharpener. Pencils are 100 times better than pens as they last that many times as long. It's probably an urban myth but the story goes that in the space race the USA spent loads of dollars developing a pen that would work without gravity. The Russians just took a pencil. I imagine those pencils that went to Outer Space are worth a good few Rusky roubles, I'd love to own one and will profess to having one if ever I'm interviewed about my writing. Why let the truth get in the way of a good anecdote?

I imagine the interviewer saying, 'What influences your writing?' and responding, 'My pencil because it sends my writing into Outer Space, which interestingly is where it's been, as it was previously owned by a cosmonaut!'

## Keeping busy, busy, busy...

I've got a busy evening ahead with my next workout, I need to exert excess energy with my bipolar condition, it's good for anyone's mental health to exercise but for me, especially in here, it's essential. I continue to hear the slang of the neighbours. Razor Smith was commissioned by Penguin to write a book of prison slang but he's old skool, having last served a sentence in the 1990s. As you know by now, my family is from Everton, the part of Liverpool nearest the docks. The accent is different from the rest of that city. I wonder if in Liverpool jails the slang is delivered in a scouse accent. How many grime artists are from Merseyside?

On my medication mission and DENIED the library, the only books on my cell table are on the Christian religion, not something I believe in and not of interest, for now, so I lucked out in that prison literature lottery. There is lots of luck in prison, but it's mainly bad luck. Maybe God's trying to find me, he has been known to find many prisoners but for me not today. On my last sentence I did contemplate becoming a Muslim, but only because

Muslims get their canteen goodies on Thursdays, a day early, because Friday is the Muslim day of rest. Other prisoners of whatever religion must wait till Friday, and in the case of canteen consumables on skint Thursday it can be the longest 24 hours of the week.

### The Gaza Strip

At the medication counter, I chat to an Asian lad, 26-years-old and back inside after being out of this hotel for only eight weeks. In the UK you are three times more likely to go back to prison once you've been inside. The reason for his return was a row with the missus that led to the police being called to their flat, and them taking him back to the station, which triggered his recall to prison. This is, without doubt one of the main reasons many heterosexual prisoners are in the system, far more than the second reason, drug offences. Relationships like those I describe in *Chapter 5* where the couple had a row and either the neighbours called for the police or the missus did. I didn't ask him which one called the police as I felt it was indiscreet, in the criminal world discretion is everything. Loose lips sink ships. The system delivers anger management courses. It really should add Relate* as a training provider.

The Asian lad asks what medication I'm on and tells me what he takes for his ADHD. He advises me to get onto A Wing where he was a resident last time round, as it is much more settled with longer serving prisoners. Most prisons have five wings named using letters. He says wings B, C, D are like the Gaza Strip with robberies and stabbings a daily occurrence. I figure that at least there would be no shootings or bombings like in the real Gaza Strip and thank him for his 'sound advice.'

---

\*  A charity founded in 1938 that provides relationship support including counselling, therapy, mediation, training and online resources: see www.relate.org.uk

Following my golden rule of not believing everything I hear I thought I'd make enquiries of The Hustler and also prison officers whilst keeping an eye out for a suitable cellmate during exercise. One thing was for sure, this lad wasn't on my short list, his shouting and banging from his cell went on all day as it was, and he was four doors down. Having him as a cellmate would definitely get in the way of writing.

Dinner has just done the rounds, still with Chef's Choice till the menu sheet kicks in, more lukewarm fuel to consume rather than savour. Whilst watching 'The Chase' on TV I'm reminded of my Dad, he loves this show and it makes me think of the stress I'm putting him through by being back inside. Always remember that your family and loved ones also serve your sentence from the other side of the wall and that their fear and anxiety for your wellbeing are usually far worse than your reality. It was one of the reasons I wrote *The Little Book of Prison*, to help families understand what happens in the first few days and weeks of someone entering the prison system.

### Making the most of time out

As I did last time I was incarcerated, I will treat prison as a health farm. You can lose a few pounds and get loads of early nights. Most prisoners come out looking much better physically than when they went in, sadly, mentally speaking, each and every prisoner will I think come out worse, especially under the COVID regime.

On National Prison Radio it's the Gay Pride celebrations today. They are asking inmates what they're doing to join in. My bipolar brain begins to imagine a 'Touching Your Toes Competition' in the showers as a potential activity. I've only seen prisoners performing the swagger as they go up and down the wing, no parading that I can see today, no rainbow flags or pink latex chaps with the arse missing, or purple cowboy hats.

I've had a visit from Jason, a healthcare worker. He has worked in prisons for ten years. He's a sub-contractor to the prison service and he went through a basic checklist to establish my wellbeing. This is a prison procedure, a failsafe paper exercise to establish that you are not about to self-harm or commit suicide. We have the highest suicide rate we've ever had in prisons and that was pre-COVID. I fear that this more brutal regime will only accelerate these fatalities. The exercise will protect the establishment if a suicide happens, they will be able to say that the paperwork they completed showed no signs of suicidal thoughts.

This HMP Hotel has around 800 prisoners with a third of the population suffering from a mental health condition. The healthcare unit has around ten beds none of which are available until you've self-harmed or attempted to kill yourself, only then will they make space, to the detriment of existing occupants who will be put back into the general prison population prematurely. A lose-lose situation for every at-risk prisoner but this has been the status quo for far longer than Jason's tenure.

While Jason ticked his boxes I was busy trying to get him to push for emergency phone credit so I could call my loved ones, trying to get something useful out of the exchange. After he left, I wondered if he really cared about the mental health of prisoners. His attitude didn't seem like it, but who knows, he was going through the motions and praying for answers that didn't expose the severe and gaping healthcare provision.

Another positive today is the weather. It's been a roasting summer so far. I reckon I lost a few pounds on the fun bus three hours sardine tin rigmarole. Today it's cooled down which is a result. My 7 pm workout will be slightly easier and should help the discipline in doing it as I'm aching today. Discipline is key but is a word I struggle with, along with other words like routine and schedule, sadly these are not just words on the page but the reality of my stay for the coming months. Watching these words coming off my pencil onto the paper confirms my reluctance to comply but one day at a time will have to do.

There is a breeze outside, which converts into a trickle of air coming through the one vent next to my cell window. This only opens an inch but is the single source of fresh air. Apparently, A Wing actually has windows. If the draft from the slit isn't enough to cool me down the alternative is to lie on the floor and enjoy the slight draft of stale air from the half-inch gap below the cell door. To be honest there's very little in it, a bit like the amount of fresh air in your shoebox that has been taken-up with the smell of the Chef's Special.

My medication is now 'in possession' (meaning in my own hands). Rather than having to take it in front of the nurse at the healthcare hatch, I can now do so at my leisure. Freedom is a wonderful thing.

I can hear prisoners getting moved on and off the wing, new arrivals, and 14-day COVID graduates, giving a fresh rhythm to the HMP soundtrack. It seems there is a domestic going on next door, another example where she rang the police and he got recalled and put back inside. Luckily his phone credit is minimal, so his screaming rant is short lived. He's now chatting through the vent to his neighbour, about the missus and his neighbour, who is shouting back a similar story. The phrase, 'Oh my days' is used by both of them to emphasise their reactions to their missuses ringing the police, not too discreet these two.

This expression has been around a while as I heard it used on my last sentence. Maybe I should try it. 'Innit right brudda, safe fam, chatting shit,' or not. I think you already know the answer to that one.

## Just a number

I've just been counted by the evening officer on his walkaround. The flap was opened, I was observed in my unnatural habitat and it was closed. I'm just another prison number, in fact the very same one I was issued with nine years ago. Makes sense and saves on paperwork for your second and third visits as the statistics shape the administrative process.

My second workout is done. I think it went a little quicker thanks to the hard house tunes, my legs feel like jelly, I'm like Richard Prior in the film 'Stir Crazy' a classic comedy where he and Gene Wilder are framed for a bank robbery and sent to jail to serve 125-year sentences. In the scene that mirrors my current exhaustion, Prior calls out for his pillow on the top bunk after a long day of hard labour, he can't reach it and ends up pulling the mattress on top of himself. The next morning when the guards wake them he is still on the floor. If you've never seen the film go to YouTube and find this clip, I find it hilarious.

I've finally made it into my cosy prison crib, it is still a surreal feeling. I have spent 72 hours at HMP Hotel and have tried not to make sense of my situation yet. In truth I'm still not ready to face-up to its madness but I can reflect that since COVID the whole world has gone into lockdown and I take heart that, for now at least, I'm still breathing.

# Chapter 8

Freedom of the Bipolar Mind

It's difficult to be a humorist when you're the only one laughing! I'll not try to explain the joke, nor attempt to persuade anyone that it's funny or (in truth) tragic. It is laugh, or cry, is it not?

## Expressing myself safely

I've always played the fool as it can lower the defences of others and create a connection with them. The spirit that is most free will always sing the sweetest notes and, with the capability to create the most inspiring of lyrics (or the most morose) you hold the power to manipulate the listener's emotional condition — understanding that this is a responsibility, and should be delivered with care. What I now know, in my dotage, is to commit my thoughts through the pencil (and onto the page) where they are expressed safely. Anyone is welcome to pick-up these words if they serve a purpose for them — if they find them of any use whatsoever. If anyone finds them worthless then, so-be-it. I have no feelings other than a wholehearted respect for their opinion.

## Autopilot

Defiance and love are truly weapons we possess to keep our minds free in the battle of wills, fighting against the faceless dark forces infecting society with prescribed thinking. These subtle manipulators attempt to control our minds through caustic values, silently injected into our souls to nullify the human spirit. They create a thick fog of insecurity that confuses our convictions and erodes our confidence forcing us to question our self-belief. The aim is to induce a waking coma, so we are sleepwalking through their influence, and they are dictating the choices we think we make in our own lives.

Only the rare few can resist being seduced by this dark and demonstrative dogma, with every breath they stay the course of freedom of thought. It takes courage to resist where most fail, to hold on to your moral compass as this force summons a fog within the mind that thickens like rotten propaganda you are blinded by and forced to inhale.

Dark clouds of control create a storm of bondage and illusion smashing hailstones against their resolve and sheet-lightning that blinkers their vision, in an attempt to blur their view of sinister purpose. The rare few can endure the storm with strength, love, freedom of spirit, and integrity of the soul to defy the black waves of an oppressive tide that never retreats, never subsides and only swells to drown free will.

The strongest of us may keep our heads above water for years, fight against the relentless power of the storm for decades, winning each battle of wills, but at the cost of weakening our resolve as the war rages on and the rip tides of nuance and suggestion create unseen currents with ever more power to drag the human spirit from the light into the depths of eternal darkness and confusion. Only the rare few realise it is best not to fight but to rise above it, without expelling effort, accept the barrage and float on its surface. Able to breathe they are safe from the danger just inches below. Living on the edge is where you'll find these few—their lives are lived to the limit every single day, with vigour, with purpose and a humility that uses the force against itself.

For the poor souls who live in fear of this power they are at its continued mercy as the dark force is constant and tireless in attacking the human spirit. Assaults are meticulously planned, to perfection, and deviously implemented by proxy to unknowing agents under hypnotic control. No longer using traditional methods of attack, they infect through channels far less obvious but much more effective, an unassuming tyranny. They are craftsmen of this weaponry and formidable in using it. Their ancestors have waged conventional war for centuries, their successors are now trained in the darkest arts of guerrilla warfare. They attack the mind into submission through manipulation that in most cases goes unnoticed by the victims.

This power does not offer to buy your soul, to conduct a fair and honest trade, even the Devil has the scruples to play a fair game. This evil steals without consent and hides in plain sight. It is able to be smuggled past our traditional defences like a smiling assassin to claim ownership of our most precious of all human possessions. It plunders so quickly that we have no knowledge of it, a masterthief in black cotton gloves, leaving no marks to signal it was ever there. Only over time do we come to realise that we have an emptiness within, the feeling that something inside us is missing, the saddest reality is not knowing what has been taken. Never being able to replace what has been lost, irreversible as time, our demise is slow and painful, as the human spirit implodes until we are spent and perish.

But this heinous crime cannot be committed against the rare few in the same way, those that can see them for what they are, those that have the sensory perception to feel them nearby and prepare when they get within reach. A warrior spirit lies within each of the rare few. The heart of a lion, fearless and formidable in battle without ever being shown techniques or trained for the moment. The rare few fight back on instinct and take the fight to the attackers, their life force is aimed at the black hearts of these thieves, it enters and on impact explodes leaving only black ash and dust that is blown to the furthest corners of their domain. There they are reborn, retrained, and sent back into battle, driven by greed, and lusting more control, insatiable for more power. The war rages on, the casualties increase and the rare few continue the fight, as it has been from the beginning and as it will be at the very end of human existence. Once extinct they will move to another time in another place, with another species raging the same war using the same weapons, craving the same foul end game. There are such things as evil beings that control the doers of evil deeds.

Apologies for the shift in writing style and its content. The worth of this writing is insignificant, with the message defined by the reader and the position contrived. During this process, my bipolar brain goes into a trance-like state and the words pour out of me without having to think at all — as if guided by some nonsensical autopilot. The end product is something I never know what to make of, but there it is, jettisoned from me and found by you.

## Rebuilding a broken life

I've been on this planet for 50 years — half a century sounds even longer — and, if written in Roman numerals, looks yet more ancient! I've been lucky enough to study at university in my mid-20s and again as a postgraduate in my thirties. The timing of my academic education and the motivation to learn were critical to staying the course and in completing the journey. My ex-wife might say it was the worst thing I ever did, but we have always begged to differ in our contentions, conclusions and thinking. Who is to say if she is right and I am wrong, as ignorance of education could be bliss to some?

My first prison experience was attained through the hypermanic episodes and misadventures of a severely unwell man, a man undiagnosed of his bipolar condition and unable to comprehend why his self-destruction was happening so fast that the world was crashing down behind him, not around him. Fortunately, with the help of finally being sectioned under the Mental Health Act, being diagnosed and medicated to help control my condition, and my acceptance of being bipolar, I could then focus on the long, hard road to recovery with the tools to rebuild my life. During this journey, or as I would put it, the process of 'getting back to my best,' I had the precious time (and even more precious family and friends support network) to re-evaluate my past and plan my future. Similar to what the population of the world is having to do with the global COVID pandemic.

What I know now is that even in the most severe tests in life come some poignant and enlightening life lessons. A kind of rebirth that has given me passion and commitment to contribute positively to my community by doing everything I can to help others. I am not religious so do not follow or fear the teachings or wrath of God, Allah, Buddha, Brahma, or Waheguru alongside the other 9,995 deities of the world. I am a humanist guided by my heart.

I'm sure that I'm not a conformist, I'm not a socialist and I'm certainly not a capitalist. I have wasted far too much time in police cells, been productive in prisons, and subscribed to treatment in mental hospitals. I have taken drink and drugs to excess both illegal and everyday pharmaceuticals, but I am not an addict to any. I have an extrovert personality and an excessive nature alongside a boredom threshold that leaves excess before irreparable damage is inflicted to find something new no matter what the substance or liquid consumed or exercise routine, sport, or pastime I focus my attention on.

The only constant that has been with me for the last 40 years is writing and even then it follows no real pattern and is fluid like my bipolar condition and (as in life) full of ups-and-downs, ebbs-and-flows.

In terms of belonging, my sense of self is not aligned to typical persona, no style of living, no membership of a group, gang or tribe, nor socio-economic cohort. I'm for the most part nondescript. I can tell you that I leaned more toward Mods than Rockers, more to New Romantics than Punks, and I am more pacifist than football hooligan, more leader than a follower, immune to most peer group pressure but intolerant of those that impose their will on others. I understand the need for law and order but I'm guilty of ignoring it on occasion even when in good mental health. I'm interested in Psychology, intrigued by the strength and power of the mind and by the dangers of the weak-minded and their programmed bigotry, beliefs they are powerless to challenge, values that can be deployed into damaging actions on their fellow men and women in their communities, manifesting in physical and mental abuse through uncontrollable bias. I am however a victim of one thing that shapes my persona, that then projects to the world or the portion of it in front of me.

## Defiance and enrichment

Being defiant is more challenging than being bipolar, it takes huge energy and focus, it is something that encapsulates me. A thing that comes from my very core and I believe has been with me since my inception, in my inherent nature, not derived from my nurtured experiences in early life. It takes determination and drive to question the polite structures of acceptance, to be strong enough to repel the guilt and scorn of the majority. To challenge all and any rule of perceived acceptability or supposed standards in which we are expected to place ourselves. My bipolar brain will not give me the logic that most people find easy to understand, and even easier to follow.

I have a societal IQ of zero — perhaps even a minus rating would be more apt. I am unable to do the simplest of things, to conform to a pre-devised pattern of acceptable conduct and unquestioning following of standards and constructs. At the heart of this affliction is the issue of effective communication, expressive perception, and the pure joy of debating the worth of perceived social rules and restrictions.

My resistance is relentless. I am not a product of my environment — I have not evolved over 50 years in my defiance — rather spent the years up to the fall from grace and then my rebirth biting my tongue until I bled to death over-and-over, time-after-time. Behaving as people would expect me to, to please people, to make people feel comfortable, and all the while thinking that something wasn't quite right but resigned to the fact that I must be at fault.

My communication is seen as negative, argumentative, only by those who bleat their opinions as if they were orders on how you must apply reason to comply with rules to live your life by. Incapable of grasping that all points of view and opinions are equally valid and can only come from knowledge, not the lack of it. To use your brain to its full potential can only be realised with an open mind and loving heart that enables you to learn, leading to a better understanding of differing points of view. We have all heard the term 'salt of the Earth' and yet it has never been formerly explained to most people.

Most writers born after the Renaissance period were able to put their thoughts into the hands of the people that writers' characters were based on, most writers I identify with base their stories on their own experiences, from a knowledgeable standpoint. The broader the scope of the writer, the more inclusive they became to a wider audience, and yet I would argue that their best work was always based on the lives of the salt of the Earth. Then as now the wealth and power of the modern world is owned and controlled by a small fraction of the total population who are shielded from the harsh and brutal realities of life.

Having a social conscience is not popular, voicing it even less so, something I have learned the hard way. It causes more challenges than solutions, presents more questions than answers. To share my inner voice by setting it on a page is a healthy and creative thing. But giving a commentary to those who have not asked for it will always fall, in the main, on very deaf ears and I respect that, and yet that is what Government and commerce continuously bombard us with 24/7 as citizens and consumers in what is deemed to be a civilised society.

But I have the inner fear that, to some people, their sensibilities can make them block out logic and reason. I think a solid purpose is to contribute something that can bring enrichment to our society and serve the people within it, surely nurturing our sense of belonging to ourselves and to one another is a human need that has been neglected for far too long. We are said to be more connected through technology than at any point in human evolution and yet we have never felt so alone. Fuelled by crass ambitions to be more superior, more successful, and more important than others, which only serves to drive people apart not bring them closer together.

If I could ask one thing of everyone, one thing for them to consider, it would be to think about our current trajectory and what the future will look like, then think how our children's futures will turn out. I would ask everyone to make freedom of thought part of our lives, something we should never subdue. This in my humble opinion is far, far more progressive than freedom of speech which seems to focus more on being heard. I would move the focus instead onto the more valuable and inclusive commodity of listening.

We have been and will always be at odds with ourselves and each other. It's a fragile weakness of human nature we all possess. Arguments and disagreements are constant with people who come from the same culture, let alone from different ones. How do we expect to reach a more harmonious human existence on the current trajectory? On the other hand, some people believe the sum of our life has no meaning at all, next to the lifetime of the planet our mortality is a millionth of a millisecond of the Earth's existence.

But in this insignificant time, almost every one of us takes more from the planet and causes more damage than we give back, repair, or improve. We simply fail to take responsibility for our part in Mother Nature's demise as if she doesn't care for us. If so, can we realise that we need to care for each other before it is too late?

## Sid Vicious and the man in the street

If life has no meaning—then to those who believe this—I say have a good time all the time, laugh and love as often as possible, run up as much debt with banks and credit card companies as humanly possible, default on payday loans, but never take from the sick, the elderly or uninsured. Use this money as a vehicle to travel in, to create anarchy, in every waking minute of every day, without exception.

Remember the immortal words of Sid Vicious an anarchist of nobility, the Prince of Chaos, and in his day Public Enemy No.1, a hero of free-thinking, free-will, and carnage. His reign was short but in the late-1970s his status was the undisputed Champion of Anarchy. To use a football analogy, if Sid was one of the competing teams he'd have won the Champions League, the Premier League, the FA Cup, the Charity Shield, the Mickey Mouse Cup, and would have set the record for most red cards ever. He was at the top of his game, in a different class, a league of his own. I would have loved to have borne witness to his craft.

In his moment he was interviewed by a seasoned music journalist (a serious commentator and when I say 'serious' he was well-respected in the industry, so he thought a lot of himself out of respect for the industry thinking a lot of him). The interview went like this:

Journalist: 'So, Sid, The Sex Pistols stage performance carries the angst of the younger generation—your lyrics speak to, and understand, the man in the street. Do you and the band think about the man in the street when you create your lyrics?'

Sid Vicious: (looking thoughtful, rubbing his chin, possibly high and contemplating his answer, then speaking calmly and eloquently, like a tea-total professional): 'No, as I have met the man in the street and he's a cunt.'

He then appears to have assaulted the journalist with a bicycle chain before going about his anarchical business. Ironic (on many levels) as music is a place where you can free-think, can say the unspeakable, think the unthinkable, challenge the Establishment and people will listen and further may be influenced. Sid turned this on its head, saving his best work (and worst behaviour) for when he was simply being himself, as he sang 'I want to be Anarchy.'

# Chapter 9

## Where There's Life There's Drugs

Yes, where there is life there will always be drugs so far as I can predict. The proportion of UK prisoners with a drug problem has doubled in the last five years with more than 60 per cent of heroin users admitting that they used whilst in the prison system. I can tell you heroin is not available on the canteen sheet.

In the UK one in eleven youngsters and adults aged 16-to-59 years has taken an illegal drug, that is around 60 per cent of the population. Legal pharmaceuticals are used by 99.9 per cent of society and are as basic a need as food, water and shelter in the modern Western world. We are hugely overmedicated and painfully under educated, in my humble opinion.

Our emotional need is to live a healthy and happy existence where illegal drugs are not needed nor consumed, but it seems to me that they are sought after by a very large part of society and perhaps for most are enjoyed safely for recreation, stimulating social interactions and promoting happy wellbeing and purpose, not in an attempt to become addicted, commit a crime or a resident of HMP Hotel.

The national opinion on drugs is shaped by those who govern drug use in society, manufacture drugs and the media that only seems to comment on negative and extreme impacts. The opinion I always value the highest is that of the drug user and their family and friends when they talk from personal experience. Ask the man or woman in the street and be sure you're get differing opinions. Depending upon which street he or she resides in.

## Public opinion

I'm always fascinated by opinions and how they are structured by a mixture of personal experience and media influence. The critical factor for me is consumption, is it the use or the abuse of drugs which shapes our strongest beliefs? Some will say they're a plague, that drugs create crime and kill people. This is usually in reference to illegal drugs. On a different street, the response could be that drugs take away pain and suffering, give a better quality of life, prolong life expectancy, and allow more mobility so people can live a more full and active life. Usually in reference to lawfully prescribed drugs.

However, you can bring together the views of very different streets if you frame the question differently. For example, by asking 'Why do you think people abuse drugs and what happens when people get addicted?' Then the legal drugs begin to threaten people's lives, as now the shift has presented a problem in their community (when a topic is closer to home this seems to make a difference to what people think about it), but even then, the consumer's abuse is still not seen to cause crime, well not directly anyway. Then please ask, 'Do you think drugs are too expensive? Do you think suppliers exploit the consumer for profit?'

The answer from both streets will be the same: 'YES they are and YES they do.' There is a mindset of 'Why should we, the taxpayers, spend more than we absolutely have to so as to make sure drugs are available to those that need them, especially when financed from our own pockets' (legal drugs). The sentiment is the same, as to why we should not be overcharged by suppliers who reduce the purity of the drug to increase profits, ingest cutting agents that are harmful and lead users to have to buy twice to get the required amount (illegal drugs). I would say that suppliers of illegal drugs always exploit their customer base and believe we should guard against the supply of legal drugs being determined, e.g. by the need to satisfy investors.

Most if not all drugs derive from natural substances, Mother Nature's gifts that exist in most if not all cultures and come largely from plants and very occasionally animals. Each substance must be treated with the respect it deserves and should never be taken to excess. Drug control is dictated by the society it serves, guided historically by ancient cultures and nowadays by modern-day research, with the aim of preventing abuse. Whether brilliant but 'inconvenient' findings concerning the benefits or dangers of (often naturally occurring substances) is always accepted or followed by policy-makers seems to be a different story.

Myrrh is considered one of the earliest natural drugs, recorded and written down by practitioners on tablets (blocks of stone or wood not something to be swallowed or used to surf the internet!) dating back to 2600 BCE. Myrrh was used to treat coughs, colds and inflammation, considered by society at the time as 'safe' to use and not seen as a problem for crime levels or the death toll of its users. It was also promoted, to a degree, by religious writing as when the parents of baby Jesus were given some by a wise man, or so the story goes. Just because it was written down does not make it gospel, well not to a non-believer. Assuming the story is true you can ascertain that it was at the time considered safe for babies to be around at least.

### More lessons from history

The Egyptians listed around 700 plant-based drugs in 2900 BCE yet interestingly they now ban pharmaceutical opioids from their country, with prison sentences in years not months if you are caught in possession of them. The powers that be, the guardians of the population, feel that opioids are highly addictive and destructive to their society. They have taken away the legal choice of consumption from the people while at the same time purchasing and administering the banned drug within their healthcare system. To treat the very same people they feel cannot be trusted to self-medicate.

My personal favourite is the Middle Ages record on drugs. Where they derive from and instructions on safe manufacture and consumption were held in monasteries by monks (until these 'pharmacies' were seized by King Henry VIII along with any other valuables they owned). The word 'addict' comes from the Latin *addictus* translating as devoted sacrifice. I bet you never saw an unhappy monk and I imagine the local population thought this was because of their serenity rather than their close possession of the keys to the medicine cupboard.

The Arabians seem have been the first to allow privately owned pharmacies to dispense drugs to the populace from the eighth century onwards. The owners were a blend of physicians (doctors), philosophers (hippies) and poets (musicians and writers), very different styles of management combined with that of the country and culture they resided in, but all with the same disposition. Funded by the powerful who profited from the poor, who were the majority of the customer base. Those who managed the pharmacies were extremely successful in attracting customers and my bipolar brain makes me wonder if they freely consumed the fruits of their own labours.

### White coats

Alongside the above mode of delivery was the holistic approach where prescriptions were not written down or substances sold for profit. These equally respected sources were perhaps more knowledgeable, aficionados of their products and their potencies and only ever represented the drugs within their realm, specialists rather than general practitioners with limited, passed-down knowledge.

I suppose its hard for a modern-day GP to keep tabs on all legal or illegal drugs any more than developments in mental health, cardiology, orthopaedics or 101 categories of healthcare. Even with the modern focus on mental suffering we maybe still have a long way to go before more answers are available in every local doctors' surgery.

Mental ill-health has always been identified through history, but since the 17th century (the Age of Enlightenment) madness was increasingly seen as an organic physical phenomenon, no longer involving the soul or moral responsibility. Holistic deliverers were immersed in cultural expertise when dispensing drugs, they were revered for their spiritual power that stemmed from the human spirit and the soul, rather than benign and detached educational credentials. Their position of authority was above reproach, adhered to without the need for a uniform. With great power comes far greater responsibility. They had a deep ethical responsibility to drug administration and members of society. They wanted their society to thrive and grow equally in mind, body and spirit, not create addiction and crime.

### Trial and error

Knowledge of medicinal plants turned into palatable uses by trial and error over hundreds of years. These not-so-clinical trials tested crude formulae on the poor, the criminal, and the abandoned. In Victorian times this may still have been the *modus operandi*, using relatively poor people in trials to develop the final drugs that were in a safe state to then allow rich people to use them without risk. A sound commercial position as the aim was to maximise profit (sorry ... and to make people better). Killing the rich customer base can be problematic to the bottom line of a business; killing poor people is not it seems an issue to the more unscrupulous.

Investors in legal drug companies can see themselves as philanthropists first, second as patrons of profit, investing their monies into companies that work toward a greater good caring for humankind. Drug company profits in the US alone were $548 billion in 2020. Its all about helping people (even if some investors may be less philanthropic) and to do this there are nowadays extensive safeguards around clinical trials, many volunteers are paid and stringent controls exist (at least in the UK and other advanced nations). Nonetheless we should be wary and demand the highest standards of any drug used on the human mind, in particular. Do forgive me if my bipolar condition makes me quick to develop conspiracy theories.

In terms of opioids alone in recent years I'm told that over 100,000 people in the USA died from opioid overdoses each year and sadly this figure increases by 20 per cent year-on-year. To put that another way, more Americans were killed by opioid overdoses in the past two years than died in the Vietnam War.

## Prohibition

Drugs have been categorised and classified for the past 50 years in the UK in a vain attempt to either demonstrate their perceived (though sometimes contentious) destructive ability to our society or for the legal framework to inform criminal sentencing and judicial guidelines. They include heroin, cocaine, marijuana, LSD, MDMA (ecstasy) amphetamines, hashish, magic mushrooms, opiates, barbiturates and ketamine. The provisions are complex and often illogical but generally the supply, possession or manufacture of these (and other drugs) is prohibited via often severe criminal sanctions, though some can be prescribed by doctors or vets in strictly controlled situations.[*]

---

[*]    For an up-to-date account and changes over time in terms of prohibition, classification of given drugs and views on relative harm, see *Drug Science and British Drug Policy: Critical Analysis of the Misuse of Drugs Act 1971* (Waterside Press, forthcoming).

It was only around 100 years ago that the Western world decided to make some drugs lawful and some drugs unlawful ('drug control' which differs across international jurisdictions). In 1915 to be precise. It begs the question whether if they knew then what we know now would this have happened at all? In effect, this decision made holistic delivery a criminal offence, tricky if you're a Druid at Stonehenge practising your Pagan rituals or celebrations.

Sadly, this outdated thinking has remained law and fuels the prison population. The UK political approach to tackling drugs in society is no longer fit for purpose; the vain hope is that longer and longer sentences will resolve the root cause of why certain substances and their consumption rates cause chaos in the community.

Portugal is, in my opinion, approaching drug use in society from a mature and moral standpoint. It has decriminalised all drugs since 2001 and interestingly drug use is way below the UK average. In Portugal the highest decline in users is amongst those aged 15–24 years. Every year less and less of the general population take drugs.

All countries that enforce drug laws have only a marginal impact with hugely expensive costs to police this. Whereas in other countries where drugs are lawful the harm of illegal drug use to societal health has been dramatically reduced, plus HIV and hepatitis levels have also tumbled creating less cost to their healthcare systems. Crime rates have fallen along with drug-related offences and prisoner populations have been halved.

The Global Commission on Drug Policy is a high-level group of former leaders in Government, civil society, and business. To their mind, the focus should be on prioritising harm reduction and promoting the decriminalisation of drugs. I'm positive that within my lifetime we will see this become a reality, but I fear that the UK will be one of the last to reform its drug laws and our society will be the poorer for it.

# Chapter 10

Illiteracy: The Inescapable Truth

---

If outmoded drug laws are a cause of crime (*Chapter 9*) here is another. In the UK, 48 per cent of prisoners can't read. Across society it is estimated at eight million adults. Both share the same illiteracy, the same disadvantaged background, hard upbringing, and poor life experiences. One of our biggest strengths in the university sector is international students choosing the UK, based on our reputation for excellence in delivering education. I understand that: we play to our strengths. But I would ask, 'What focus is there on tackling this huge weakness, which excludes and creates problems for so very many?'

### Isolation and deprivation

If you are illiterate you are isolated from society, not only deprived of knowledge and education but most likely from a deprived area, upbringing and connected to social services, abuse, and childhood trauma. Your parents are likely to be illiterate, unemployed, with addiction issues, and to have committed crime.

When your circumstances are so impoverished—and your outlook is bleak—then often so are your choices. Such people have my deepest sympathies and understanding, especially when they see it with their own eyes. It is something they did not deserve; it was their fate and without remedy even though we have the tools to end it.

I find it hard to be proud of our education system that has helped me to grow but has left others that need it the most in the darkness of illiteracy. Circumstance leads to an unconventional life, with coping mechanisms that are ingenious, imagine adding literacy to these achievements, imagine the potential for transformation.

As a literate prisoner, I know that books can be a beautiful relief from incarceration or a poison chalice if they don't spark an interest, at least I am gifted to be able to make that distinction. In a police cell in hypermanic March I was introduced to Daphne du Maurier's classic novel *Rebecca* and it took me on a journey. I read it cover-to-cover in one sitting as the story unfolded and my fingers flicked the pages to reach the twist in the tale.

## Eternal suffering

I packed several books in my 'just in case I'm sent to prison case.' They are stacked on my desk as I write, but I've yet to be in the right frame of mind to pick one out. I'm now the proud owner of another book from my last excursion down the wing. It's a work entitled *The Buddha's Path to Deliverance*. I know a little bit about this religion and read some Zen Buddhism in my enjoyably misspent college days.

The Buddha said, 'One who is willing to attain Nirvana has to understand Four Noble Truths. These are the key to attaining Nirvana: proper understanding of Suffering, Cause of Suffering, Relief of Suffering, and the Way to end Suffering. Who knows I may have a chance of reaching Nirvana unless COVID prison time doesn't qualify as suffering? I'll consult the Buddhist when he turns up at my door and ask him if the eternal suffering of illiteracy may qualify also.

There is much to be said about the experience of reading, with this gift I am free to inhabit someone else's life, in my own time, giving me the choice of how deep to go. I have a passport to lead the life of another being either real or fictional (but ultimately what is the difference to the experience?). It's a mental holiday to visit another person's mind, soul, and spirit. It's not like TV or a film, it takes work, focus, and concentration—but you're rewarded for your efforts in a way more unique and whole than any other experience. Although in the end, after all the words are consumed and nurtured, you will always end up being yourself. Just with more knowledge and more freedom of thought.

From experience, I can tell you that from desperation can come inspiration. The Brazilian painter Cesar Cruz said, 'Art should comfort the disturbed and disturb the comfortable.' He has my heartfelt thanks. I feel the same about my own writing.

This teleportation in words on the pages of books, each bound together down the left hand side is just a few feet from me. Most books I see there are ones I really want to read, but they're all neglected for now. I have noticed some more in the corner of the ground floor of the wing, I wonder what they might be, will they give me any joy or vital escapism? Ultimately, will I commit to the discipline to enter each of those worlds, or even to enter any?

I like to think that in being so very alone I can choose to belong to another world, I am so lucky to be able to read, I cannot imagine not having that luxury, and it makes me feel sad to know that there are millions of people in society that have been let down by our revered education system.

## Saturday

Well, dear reader, 'Happy Saturday.' No need for an alarm clock, the banging of doors as the breakfast packs are delivered serves as my wake-up call around 8 am. How thoughtful. UB40 are on National Prison Radio singing 'If it happens again, I'm leaving.' Like having a massive, unpleasant thought of 'never again' as you come round to the reality of a second prison stay. Well, second time unlucky, and I truly hope that this time will be the last time. I was thinking of the lad yesterday who described other wings as like the Gaza Strip. In HMP on my first sentence they called B wing Beirut. Jails are jails and porridge is porridge: cold, grey and with so many lumps you find it hard to swallow.

There is a definite need for prisoners to tell things to fellow inmates who they know from their local area. Standard stuff I suppose, and prison is scary so any kind of acceptance of knowing people ('peeps' in prison slang) can hold the hope of friendship and might lower the chances of either party getting robbed, stabbed, or both. It may possibly be even more needed due to the prolonged isolation under COVID. The feeling of being alone is for some worse than the feeling of being locked-up. Fear is ever-present on the wing, but for some isn't that life, when they live with mental health challenges, hopelessness, helplessness, anxiety, and fear greeting them every day they wake up? But nothing competes with the eternal torture of GUILT. Put the two together and you can understand why we have the biggest prison suicide rate we've had for 30 years.

On the positive, it's much cooler today and has rained overnight and its exercise for me but sadly no 20-minute tan top-up outside. Prison life is a lottery, an empty box of chocolates, or maybe a circus that you don't just watch but perform in. Yes, you guessed it, I'm in with the clowns. Things can always be worse. If it was a winter sentence my medication and age would make me feel the cold much more. So I should think myself lucky.

I managed to set out some work yesterday but as its Saturday do I take the day off, or do I keep up the momentum? It's a rest day from the workouts, so I'm leaning toward reading a book and watching the telly. I'm not sure I can stop writing though, it feels therapeutic as it was on the last sentence, I think I may have an acute condition called 'scribe's fever.'

What if I couldn't read or write? Can you imagine how much smaller my world would be? The first ex-offender I ever taught to read was in his late twenties, a big lump with more than a few prison stays under his belt. I walked him from probation to the library and watched as he went white as a sheet. I asked what was wrong and he replied, 'I've never been in a library before.' He could happily walk into any prison, onto any wing and feel confident. The library petrified him. I'd hardly given it a thought before that day, but I never took a learner to a library again.

The morning news is telling us how 'bleak' the economic outlook is for the rest of the year; now there's a word that speaks to prisoners, prison is the epitome of *bleak*. The vista from my window is not so bleak in fact, that's another little victory. I can see lots of nature, fields, and trees beyond the gates and walls. The old Victorian jails in city centres have nothing to look at but concrete, high walls and barbed wire. It makes a small subtle difference to your state of mind even if only slightly.

ITV4 has a show on about fishing. They're in a forest at the foot of Mount Fiji and one of the presenters has caught a big fish. He lifts it up, kisses it and says, 'Thanks for your time' then lets it go. Queer behaviour. I never really got into fishing. I would have felt a bigger sense of achievement by eating the fish and thanking its bones whilst patting my stomach. My hunter-gatherer instinct.

I never thought I would say this but I actually want time to go more slowly. I'm five workouts in and seizing-up, and not looking forward to the next one. What I wouldn't give for a bath to soak the aches away a little. I won't get a shower for the next ten days. I'm perfecting the art of the strip wash at the sink using a prison-issue T-shirt as no towels are available … Oh, the humanity. I have completed a prison app (filled in a request form) for my Mum's address and phone number to be added to my phone list so we can call each other. It's somewhere in the admin abyss of prison, anyone's guess when it might (or will ever) be administrated. Fingers and toes crossed.

It's surreal to know there is anxiety and hopelessness everywhere yet writing defo has a calming influence on me. To have a focus and a purpose is critical to dealing with a prison sentence, especially in the first few weeks and even more so in this extreme version of lockdown.

Even more surreal is learning from the news channel that, apparently, there is a UK-wide puppy shortage. People are panic buying dogs (and other things). COVID lockdown moves in mysterious ways. There are apparently websites where people are paying hundreds of pounds in deposits on puppies that don't exist. I have visions of gangs of dognappers stalking dog walkers with garden shears, going for the 'snip and grab.'

In my eccentric brain, thoughts are always happening, I just hope that when they do I have a pencil in my hand and something to write on. My brain when manic shows a sharp increase in the number of these ideas, presents more to write about, but the challenge is to stay still enough to set them down.

The last time I left prison I wasn't sure how my life would unfold; I was making sense of the worst time in my life knowing that I could never return to my old one. With this sentence I'm suffering the maximum lockdown ever delivered by the prison system, but I'm in the best position mentally to deal with it. I know my mental health condition, I have a future to look forward to, and a purpose during my time inside.

I can hear the wing cleaner's spray bottle outside my door, part of the enhanced sterilisation regime to try to combat COVID infection. I have to say that I've not felt stressed about catching COVID since coming into prison, I really haven't thought about it as I've actually felt safer in here. On the outside I didn't think I would be a victim either. My bipolar thinking didn't help of course and I joked that I was lucky to have made it to my age or even 30 so anything more was a bonus. To be vertical and breathing is a blessing that should never be wasted. I have hope in the knowledge that our minds are remarkable things. The mind can either be a wonderful servant or a terrible master. Every life, every existence is a daily battle of good and bad experiences, it's just a question of choosing what to focus on. Mental ill-health can spiral quickly downwards if you allow your mind to focus on bad experiences, it prevents you when you want to rationalise and interpret. It feeds on fears and debilitates the body's ability to breathe and begins to crush your spirit.

We are all guilty of harmful thoughts, some go further and manifest actions, none of us are pure. I'm sure that the spirit needs equal attention to guide our minds to good thoughts making us feed on the positivity, not the negativity that we know serves no purpose. Those that suffer physical disabilities and overcome them have a human spirit that is inspirational, in such a pure and powerful form, to watch as their bottomless resolve overcomes things is an example of the very best in human endeavour. The perspective it lends is overwhelming, the courage to go on infectious.

We seek the meaning of life from a position of privilege that we ignore, we motivate our life journey with the fuel of false position and unattainable perceived perfection. The truth is we are all equal in our worth and all as fragile, we all need love, support, and encouragement to grow stronger, healthier and happier. All we really need is food and water for our bodies and each other for our growth. Take heart that we are capable of extraordinary achievements if we can think and feel free, if we can comprehend that these negative pressures serve no purpose. Persevere, understand, and make sense of what is truly precious and important in our lives. You may find this is something you already possess but have never appreciated.

## Suicide Sunday

My first 'Suicide Sunday' during this ride on the incarceration merry-go-round, sadly we've the highest prison suicide rate we've ever had (*Chapter 2*). But not all suicides (or attempts) take place on this day of the week, it's just called Suicide Sunday by HMP Hotel guests because it's their longest time banged up, with only skeleton staff, so the cell door opens even less.

I can hardly move my legs this morning. I literally had to roll my body over to get out of bed. I have completed another app requesting the dentist as I have been overdue a filling for months.

I've had some work arrive through the 'Email a Prisoner Service' and have had my first post from my probation officer. I recognised her name as she has sent ex-offenders on probation orders to my reading project, the Read and Grow Society. Ironic that I'm now in the justice system and will be a service user of probation on release. The email service allows you to receive a printed copy of an email; they email the prison admin office and then the prison prints it out and delivers it like ordinary post. Some of the most important improvements in the system (such as this) come from ex-offenders fuelled by frustration and driven by a passion to help fellow and future prisoners.

The TV news is talking about parents being scared to send their children to school, I totally understand this and think they should be able to make their own decisions. Missing a few months' (even a year of) education can be caught-up on versus the prospect of infection. The Government is extending the furlough scheme (paying people most of what they would have earned) to protect businesses which, for once, I agree entirely with them about. A decision that is helpful. You don't see that very often from our leaders, but the COVID crisis has forced political power to focus on the entire population—or maybe that's just my bipolar brain.

In some sectors (I see one report says) unemployment figures will go up by five million people, the leisure sector (my sector) is taking the worst hit, and we'll all be redefining what is important in our lives. I've just seen an interview with the CEO of *The Big Issue* asking the Government to create jobs in the NHS and invest in emergency accommodation to battle homelessness. The editor is convinced that there'll be a huge surge in people falling into poverty due, as he describes it, to 'the treacle of homelessness.' He feels landlords' evictions will hit an all-time high and that this could lead to two generations of homelessness. Another boost to the prison population!

I've sent a letter to my probation officer and made a copy for my files, always wise as paperwork goes missing inside (and sometimes outside). I attempted to summarise all the relevant information to qualify for home detention curfew (HDC) on a tag and enquired who within the prison is responsible for eligibility. Anything pro-active I can do to quicken the process is well worth the effort.

My door opens and I'm offered a cell clean, another rare chance to step outside onto the landing. I walk out and I say to the officer, 'Yes please,' gesturing for him to go in and clean it himself. His facial expression goes blank, he hands me the broom and the mop. 'It's a DIY job, not a service.' So I roll-up my sleeves.

Locked back up and National Prison Radio is playing a hip-hop tune. The title is 'Locked-up' the lyrics go 'Locked-up, they won't let me out.' As if you need to be reminded of your situation you have to hear it being sung to you. My face is a picture, a grimace more than a smile and a headshake of disbelief. Fortunately, the next tune is one of Bob Marley's so I relax and sing away my disbelief, a wave of circumstance hits me hard. Now they are playing another record, for another Frankie, in another HMP Hotel. Maybe it's my alter ego or my evil twin. He has asked for another hip-hop tune. 'What's this one about? ... Being in prison.' Am I dreaming this?!

Finally, I get the chance to go on exercise out in the yard. I meet one of the boys who was on the same fun bus as me. He's from my part of the country, my sort of age and has been in and out of jail so knows the score. He like me just wants to get on with his sentence, so we talk about the possibility of sharing a cell.

They say time is money, well I'm earning 50 pence a day whilst serving my sentence, paying my dues to society. For every action, there's a reaction and, even if I'm not in my right mind I'm still the person responsible. The problem we have is that when we leave the system we continue to be punished by society, labelled, and not forgiven. Have you ever made a mistake, did you admit it, face up to it and move on? Is it fair that our mistakes should be used by society as a stick to beat us with forever? If you Google 'Frankie Owens Walking for Forgiveness' you can see the lengths I went to in order to highlight this point.

Prison is all about routine and the familiar prison soundtrack is back, I can hear keys jangling. If you're new you associate it with the hope that yours just might be the next door that opens. Once you're settled or seasoned you ignore it, well nearly, but you can't shake the whole human nature thing of wanting to be free. You can however convince your spirit to appear compliant.

# Chapter 11

## Mad Men in a Mad Cage in a Mad, Mad World

MATE … I vaped my socks off last night, my tendency to excess has been one of the reasons I'd never vaped before, my manic personality and the ease of keeping it in my mouth made me fear being constantly on it. Well, you learn something you already thought you knew every day.

### Welcome to the madhouse

A new day and new adventures. My to-do list includes adding my probation case manager to my phone credit list. The completed app then has to go into the mystical world of prison administration, and if it arrives (a fifty-fifty chance) I will be charged 20p for the privilege. As in society, surcharges and stealth taxes rob you of your wedge and those with the lowest income inevitably pay the most, welcome to the madhouse. Hopefully, my proactive approach towards contacting probation to encourage the hope of a rapid home detention curfew tag will be worth every penny.

Canteen pricing is a classic example of being robbed blind. Some items even have 'RRP £1' written on the packet that you are charged £1.40 for. It's criminal and immoral but very profitable indeed. Complaints to the National Offender Management Service about this are frequent and come from prisoners and their families as well as charities within the sector. The issue has been highlighted for a decade with the same response: statements alluding to 'A very serious and immediate investigation into every complaint.' Slow reform I can accept, but when it appears to go backwards with no acceptance or policy changes it would surely drive *you* mad as well as *me*. If you let it. Ours is a captive market in its most literal sense.

My favourite of these money spinners is telecom charges. Prisoners pay per minute to use landlines and mobiles, think 'pay-as-you-go plus part-minutes used and always rounded up.' Inflated to suit the providers and the establishment. We are abused like a drooling politician's blow-up doll, and this kind of pricing means less precious contact minutes with families and loved ones. Like the blow-up teacher, at the blow-up school with the blow-up pupils, and the blow-up headmaster who behaves like a prick to everyone and everything. He is arrested when the school and everyone in it mysteriously vanishes and is sentenced immediately by the judge who says, 'You let me down, you let the school down, you let the pupils down and I'm sending you down.' If only there was a consequence, even a rebate would suffice, I speak for every prisoner when I say it is a real 'dick move' by Government.

## Moonwalking

I had an epiphany last night. It came to me in a dream. That with every moment of adversity there is an opportunity. So, I have come to a huge life decision today, something I've run away from for years, actually it is more like decades, but finally I will do it. It will take dedication and focus but I'm going to get over this and finally I'm going to learn Michael Jackson's moonwalk. Prison's the perfect environment with its slippery floors and prison socks and I have the raw ability.

From an early age I always won disco dance competitions so I must have natural rhythm. Also, a rare collection of hideous songs, seven-inch singles on vinyl that were given out as first prize by the DJ each week. TRUST me. If a guy with white tiger print-covered speakers and three whole disco lights is giving you tunes not even he wants they are special indeed.

With no exercise or shower today I'm going for the cell workout and writing, to feed my body and mind. I may throw in some reading and a private karaoke session if NPR plays something old skool. I hear the jangling keys again but using mind over matter ignore them, I'm slowly getting the hang of only wasting my mental energy if my door actually opens.

## Round peg in a square pigeon hole

It is only when I put the kettle on that I notice the paperwork on the floor, RESULT! My emergency £5 phone credit has arrived. I will look forward to connecting with some of my nearest and dearest on a landline basis only! Also, I've been given a new label, I've been pigeonholed by the system, a box has been ticked, I'm already a prison number now I'm a socio-economic Category C prisoner (no longer a high security risk). I sit on the bunk and read the news shaking my head in disbelief at my good fortune. It's crazy but it's true to say that I'm a round peg in a square pigeonhole at best.

I did wonder whether my pirate impressions with an ornamental brass in the shape of a 17th century duelling pistol that landed me here would by the letter of the law make me a dangerous prisoner. I'm grateful and fortunate that the prison system decided the answer is no rather than the Crown Prosecution Service with its courtroom madness. Thank Heaven for small mercies. Just for fun, I thought I'd apply for my Category D status as another logical step to open conditions, day release for work, and brief but vigorous conjugal encounters. Under COVID and given my total time to serve, even without a tag, I'll be free before my December review. How mad is that?

## Extra-sensory perception

NPR is a godsend in many ways, it does a version of Radio Four's 'Thought for the Day' which is an introduction to different faiths. Slots lasting 15 minutes. I'm convinced that my bipolar condition when manic manifests in the ability to feel people's thoughts, that I can only explain as a type of extra-sensory perception. I can sense that all my fellow guests in HMP Hotel share the same thought every morning of every day which is 'For fucks sake this bloody place again' or 'What am I doing in this rat hole?' It's spooky but very real to my senses.

Today I'm learning about Paganism and its belief system. Ironically only in the prison environment do I have the time to listen with full attention, plus the allocated time slot is 11 am to 11.15 am so its undisturbed because morning exercise has ended and lunchtime is from 11.30 onwards. I lie back and listen and am intrigued by what I hear. Pure entertainment and education in a place that delivers relentless mental punishment.

Am I a Pagan? I always loved films like 'Jason and the Argonauts' and anything with Roman or Greek mythological themes. Paganism lends itself to the notion that mysticism and multiple gods exist, that rituals can unlock superhuman physical or mental abilities, that the power of witchcraft is very real and alchemy can be studied and mastered. To my hyper-active mind, it follows that in modern societal terms this leans very much toward the unexplainable and the abnormal which is where those with mental health conditions are diagnosed as delusional and unstable. That said am I displaying traits that are acceptable in Paganism and experiences that are shared by its followers? Is this logical contemplation or is it madness that floats out of my head and flows onto the page? Either way, it has sparked an enthusiastic motivation to learn more about this belief system.

A varied existence is for me a way of occupying my busy thoughts, but in my manic moments I am led by its expansive effects on my thinking. I am now focusing on more practical matters; getting a haircut from the wing barber.

It may be a relic of my years in hospitality but back then at least it paid to be presentable and take pride in your appearance. In the outside world, barbers and hairdressers are closed due to lockdown. The female population has become greyer or two-tone as hair grows out separating the reality of natural colour and exposing the costly sections from months before.

Male inhabitants have two options: let it grow and become a hippy or shave it all off and go for the skinhead look. Inside here, inside my mind, there is only the skinhead choice but there are two considerations. 'Is there a barber on the isolation wing?' and 'How much is it going to cost ... Do his services come at a telecom premium?'

Wing barber is a great job to have, allowing maximum time out of the cell and excellent opportunities for making an income and bartering. His only tool is clippers, no scissors as you may have guessed, and no interest whatsoever in whether you are happy with the finished result. Barbers on both sides of the wall are conscious of profit, my first barber was so tight he used to take the hair home and stuff his cushions with it. Honestly, ahead of his time he was in upcycling.

### Knowing the ropes

My door opens for my stroll to the meds hatch. There's a big guy in front of me that must be a new arrival. I'm surprised I've not seen more guests so far, but maybe they rotate them through the day. As I mentioned earlier in this book, mental health issues affect one in three in prison, a bigger percentage than in society. Sadly, unless you attempt to take your own life whilst incarcerated you will never get appropriate healthcare. The big guy is wearing a T-shirt and has slashed-up his arms and the cuts look razor blade deep from his wrist to his elbow. It turns my stomach to see them, but I do the usual greeting and courtesy without mentioning a thing. Self-harming is often re-offenders with a big 'prison IQ' (those who know the ropes) that are not really suffering mental health problems, a mechanism to favourable treatment by staff not a chronic symptom of self-loathing or self-destruction.

In my first year of recovery once sectioned, diagnosed, and medicated I learned as much as I was capable of under heavy doses of medication. I'd come across the phrase, 'self-harming is the body's road map of misery.' I understood completely but in here it is also deliberately used for the most basic requests from a new mattress to a kettle.

A further example of madness I've witnessed first-hand is swallowing batteries to help you get emergency phone credit or a vape kit. Without the first-hand experience of incarceration this behaviour is pure insanity, but what is most abnormal is that I understand why normal people go to such extreme lengths. We have the highest suicide rate in prison that we've ever had since records began, this is being ignored and I cannot make sense of why. The Gary Speed* tragedy stayed with me for many years as it happened when I was in recovery. On the surface he had the perfect life but was unable to cope with being alive. The preventative must be in understanding the pain that your actions will have on family and loved ones for the rest of their lives.

## Desperate times, desperate measures

This kind of knowledge hits you in the face like a sledgehammer but in desperate times people resort to desperate measures, to witness it today leaves

---

* Welsh football manager. In 2012 a coroner ruled that there was not enough evidence that he took his own life.

me feeling numb. Then as my manic mind accesses information from parts of my brain that are only available when manic I rationalise the numbness by recalling that the Egyptians, Greeks and Romans all practised bloodletting to cleanse the system.

Would a Pagan ritual that included bloodletting and a blood offering to one of the gods frame the practice of self-harm as healthy but without spiritual guidance? Why do I attempt the process of comprehending the sight of something shocking, just witnessed, and then look for a rational explanation rather than display worry and concern for the perpetrator? I'm grateful on one hand for the intellect to rationalise things and lost for words at my inability to feel compassion. It is this version of sanity that gives me comfort.

What is driving me up the cell wall is using a prison-issue T-Shirt as a towel. Again we are talking about the very basics. Being deprived of them feels so offensive that we over-react and exaggerate, not helped by the anxiety levels the system instils in us. I'm already unable to shower as the precious exercise time is crucial for trading and fresh air, now I'm being told there are no towels. It's hard not to take it personally. So instead it's time for some perspective.

I've turned on the Sky News Channel just for kicks. The COVID virus is incomprehensible to everyone in every part of the world, with the Oxford team working around the clock to create a potential vaccine. At the same time, President Trump is reported as buying-up close to the rest of the world's supply. His megalomania knows no moral bounds, he is creating a bidding war. No reports on Putin. But I would imagine he's playing the same game. One expert said, 'By attempting to compete we undermine all our strengths.' Happy 25th Anniversary Hong Kong. They should be celebrating 25 years since the UK handed back sovereignty to the people, well they are lining the streets. Guess what China got them as an anniversary present. There's a new national security law to deal with protesters which by odd coincidence carries a 25-year prison sentence. Spot on. Human rights!

Now it's time for news closer to home. The local early evening coverage live from the quarantine wing where I'm going to do my Mr Motivator meets the Green Goddess meets the Peloton, yes it's cell workout time. Prison, like COVID, has had some positives in increased physical exercise with couch to 5K increasing by 95 per cent since lockdown. Let's all go in for our first heart attack, shall we? Note to self: as Kevin my former shoe fetishist GP (*Chapter 4*) used to say, 'Better to arrive later in this world than early in the next.' I think he meant, 'Pace yourself, dear boy.'

# Chapter 12

Mystics, Fools, Writers and Mythical Beings

Since the dawn of time we've been told through different mediums—from ancient cave paintings to religious artefacts, parables to pyramids and from myths, epigrams and prophecies to old wives tales—that the world is full of mythical beings.

## Some bipolar blessings

One blessing of being bipolar is that I can contemplate the existence of these creatures, however unlikely, through educating myself. My bipolar logic can deduce that if God's holy church went on a witch hunt for nearly a century, then by that rationale if you believe in God then you also believe in witches (they are mythical beings are they not?).

I can study, I can research, and I can learn from multiple sources, from different perspectives and cultures at different points in history, from ancient times to the present day. Of course, all of this is just theorising, but gives me an informed opinion. If I choose to study Mysticism at Oxford or Cambridge as a degree topic, then a master's and a Phd, I can become an expert in the field. Dr Owens, I presume, Professor of Mythical Beings (with no practical experience whatsoever).

The beauty of hypermania is that when manic my mind is 'higher functioning' allowing me to realise that the existence of such beings, however unlikely, is also not impossible. No single human being knows with absolute certainty that they can't exist. After all Native Americans have used peyote as a religious sacrament for thousands of years to enter the spirit world. European Druid's descendants, the ancient Celts used the fly-agaric mushroom, or as those ancients called it, 'Flesh of the Gods.' It put them in direct communication with the Universe. Ancient Celts were known to be teachers, philosophers, repositories of wisdom about the natural world, and mediators between humans and gods.

In this setting I have the resources to follow the cultural guidelines, meet modern-day practitioners and gain first-hand experience of rituals. I may have the opportunity to meet or converse with a mythical being or experience the mystical oneness of all things. With this, I can now have a more rounded understanding as it gives even greater depth to my academic knowledge through cultural experience. At this point it is worth pointing out that we all have the freedom to decide for ourselves but if you are unable to grasp the concept of your own spiritual consciousness or if you have never considered it then you are oblivious to its potential existence inside all of us and in every living thing.

In the depths of a prolonged hypermanic episode the hypnotic psychosis state has led me to display behaviours that are completely alien to my core values, beliefs, and morals. When out of episode re-reading witness statements after being arrested, I can only ever compare it to Dr Jekyll and Mr Hyde. Even though many people may not have read Robert Louis Stevenson's book, the phenomenon has been told and re-told many times across many mediums, becoming an urban myth we all recognise. Two complete polar opposites (or in my case *bipolar opposites*). Completely different people.

Is it beyond the realms of all possibility that a mystical being has passed through my mind and taken brief possession of my body? Does this present one unlikely but tangible explanation backed-up by periodical evidence of other similar accounts? Having been interwoven with a mythical being in body, mind, and spirit, if only for a short time, has it left me with a connection to the spirit world? I have absolutely no idea and your guess is as good as mine but in the realms of fiction all and everything is possible.

Good examples would be J R R Tolkien's *The Hobbit* or Terry Pratchett's *Discworld*. The question is, 'Why are they so popular?' Is it because we believe in magic and mystical beings and crave to live in a world like this or is it because we do live in a world exactly like this and every reader to one degree or another knows it? The combined readership of Tolkien and Pratchett is near to the percentage of the population that suffers a mental health condition. Are these one and the same? Only those with an unorthodox mind can believe, feel, and see mythical beings, normal people lead normal lives. I often quote Charles Bukowski who I mentioned in *Chapter 2*, but it fits again here very well indeed: 'Some people never go crazy what truly horrible lives they must lead.'

### Mythical creatures

In my opinion, writers *are* mythical creatures, they don't belong to a specific time or place in history nor to one country or continent. A vehicle for knowledge or for nonsense, an educator or a fool, but equally powerful to readers as they are transformed into the mind of the writer whilst still able to control their interpretation of his or her story. Writers connect with complete strangers across hundreds of years in the same meaningful way with a velocity that jolts the spirit, that senses and shapes the mind's beliefs, speaking directly to them but multiplied by greatness (or some massive marketing budget).

People want to believe in themselves, want to be confident in what they see, what they do, and what they think they know to be true, want all of this entwined on a path that makes sense of life and gives acceptance and purpose that they can understand, can make sense of. It's usually a tangible position that creates reassurance. There is a danger in this path as you can lose sight of your life force, an energy at your centre where assurance and 'knowing yourself' exist. This value is ignored or detached as the tangible is a superficial existence, but societal acceptance can blind each and every one of us at some point in our lives. We are all guilty, but I think some, if not most, of those on this path never re-evaluate, they just blindly proceed.

I want to give you one example of my life force, my ability to share it through projecting energy to another person, a very unorthodox scenario with a powerful outcome. Sharing this with you is strange, to explain this to a mental health professional might lead to a diagnosis of delusion, and yet I am no longer afraid, I am sharing the truth of my gift.

### 'I don't get why you are here'

I walked into a pub yesterday, as I have done many times. I could feel the usual sceptical looks from the inhabitants, engineered from the superficial constructs they hold so dear, even their senses are prescribed, which is counterintuitive to their latent life force. The essence of our spiritual being has been ignored and suppressed, for me it is an energy that I absorb gratefully, I justify my theft as it is something they never use and don't realise they have ever lost, deep down they know that they once had it, the daily grind in the trenches of life has detached its existence. I don't take it all, just the first wave they are emitting from our initial contact. I can't explain why it is released by them and why it flows to me, but it is received in a peaceful and grateful way from a proximity of metres not feet.

My life journey in this very moment is unknown, I may have been led here by a lunar cycle or by the four winds, or by someone's pain. My purpose is always the same to either learn something or to help someone, but my presence is assessed, questioned, my aura and my good intentions are neither understood nor recognised from their detached spirit, but I am taking from them and waiting to transfer it. I feel empowered, my spirit is growing more powerful from the energy in the room, it does not need to be used it can simply be harvested to feed my soul.

I walk into the pub well-dressed, presentable, polite, unassuming. My movement is slow and my eye-contact with each inhabitant combined with a respectful nod and smile. I am conversing with the person behind the bar, my voice is deep for my frame but not loud, offering them a drink, being courteous, but they are closed and questioning. It creates a juxtaposition in their mind as the first impressions they have assumed are reversed by my conduct. The confusion is almost tangible, and this is picked-up by the regulars, through their eye-contact and facial expression.

I take a seat and slowly pour my bottle of ale into a half-pint glass, sooner or later I am always spoken to, never engaged at close quarters, my initial sentences are hospitable and my gesture when listening is attentive. Their inner conflict spills over from thought to speech asking the burning question everyone is thinking. My answer is honest but includes compliments about their part of the world and their pub. They accept my opening explanation, but their thoughts betray them, they do not trust me. It is as if they have an unconscious sense of my theft.

I sense that one person is drawn to me while the rest are resistant. I leave valuables at the seat, an opportunity to take them from this unwelcome stranger but knowing they will not be touched. This gambit is purposeful and increases the inner conflict of who and of why I'm here? I stand outside and the one approaches me, we face each other and the proximity by their choosing is close, they are drawn to the energy I emit that they are starved of.

I ask nothing but they pour out everything, a person I have never met says, 'Who are you, what are you doing here?' But their energy gives me multiple answers and is instantly absorbed. I sense they feel a failure, not in looks or garb but in telepathy, they do not know they are projecting and that I am receiving. I am giving attention, interest, and gratitude for their contact which is energising their life force instantly like a pleasant electric wave.

My conversation is playful, it elicits laughter and smiles which relaxes their inhibitions and opens their minds further to receive my gift. They are sharing in thought wholeheartedly while their conversation is closed and questioning. A usual comment is, 'I don't get why you are here.' My answer begins with humour, all the while my life force energy continues to flow to them, I give my final explanation. 'Maybe it was to meet you, wherever we are is exactly where we're supposed to be.'

I can never comprehend why I can feel they're so empty on the inside, lacklustre with a heavy sense of fear as if the whole world is on their shoulders. I can see they have a growing black hole that's eating their human spirit. The first gift is to be carefully removed as soon as possible but takes great mental effort and energy. The second takes even more stamina and strength to fill them with the life force, with a vitality for life. The third is to bring peace to their troubled mind, they must forgive themselves for their past actions and choices, not wallow in guilt and blame, then forgive others who have caused pain or suffering, help them to realise the harm negative thoughts have caused then empower them to focus on a positive future. From this very moment.

I wait for them to finish, I nod, smile and show intense interest in their openness and honesty. They run out of words, some faster than others, then they look at me and sigh in a long deep breath, exhale the old and the negative air. I thank them for their time but tell them I must leave as I've urgent business in the West, but part saying. 'You'll wake up tomorrow a different person.' I move slowly on to the next adventure enriched by the experience and knowledge that they will never see me again … as I was never there in the first place.

# Chapter 13

## A Tale of the (Most) Unexpected

'So now the end is near … I face the final pages.' I'm singing these words as a respectful wink to another Frank, who sold 150 million records and pioneered the concept album. The lyrics have been etched into my mind, a song I have sung with all my heart, even if a little out of key.

I hope my journey has entertained you; I feel deeply privileged that you've taken the time to think it worth your while to get to know me, hear and (I hope) learn more about my bipolar world. I've found out even more about myself, funny how writing can give the writer this most unexpected gift.

### Make your own luck!

Can we say that we make our own luck in this world? I know many men who live on the spin and gamble with a freedom of spirit and infectious fun, to them life is a game of chance, and they play the cards they're dealt. The origins of cards are fascinating, I think. An invention of ancient China during the Tang Dynasty reaching Europe in the fourteenth century. Four suits representing the four seasons, the pips on the cards add up to 365, the days of the year (the spare, second joker representing the extra day of a leap year).

I know far more people who play safe but for me they seem less free and more solemn. I can assure you that even the safe players can suffer misfortune, like the gambler, and are forced to start at their beginnings. A fresh start in life can be the best medicine, for failure teaches us the most about ourselves, but what if someone needs more than one new start? How many fresh starts is it before they are defeated by life? I would say far less than those of the gambler, in my humble opinion.

Rik Mayall and Ade Edmondson once wrote a cracking line for the characters of their sitcom Bottom about two men who found misfortune in every episode. Ade says. 'Richie, you're born, you keep your head down, then you die, and that's if you're lucky!' A gambler will never give up, will never stop believing that Lady Luck is just around the corner, all you need is the courage or lunacy to take another chance.

I like to think that we can affect the scales of fortune. I'm not superstitious but choose not to break mirrors nor walk under ladders. I do salute magpies and from time to time carry a double-headed coin but if you don't use it in the right company tails means you'll always lose even when you've hedged your bets. And yet I'm playing the odds one more time with you right now, to finish a book on *Chapter 13* is, in the publishing world, seen as courting bad luck and misfortune.

Will my honesty when writing this book bring virtue of any kind? Can an owner of a double-headed coin have virtue at all? Bryan my publisher once said that books are an unpredictable business and a best-seller a rare and beautiful thing. Like any new writer, we all have the highest hopes for our published work, for it to be legitimised by critics but, in truth, most of us want immediate fortune and fame. I guess a true writer should never look for this. Waterside is gambling I think and I hope for them it pays handsomely and for me helps mental health survivors celebrate their unique abilities, not hide them behind society's unfair and uneducated negative stereotypes. I have tried to express to you that mental breakdowns can happen to anyone, our minds are fragile rickety greenhouses, and the world pours down hailstones the size of footballs.

## Or bad luck ... and scary experiences

We've all experienced eventful lives, mine has included some events that were unwanted, unwelcome, and certainly unsavoury, but we never know where the path of life will lead us or even if we are even on the right one. Some people are dragged down a path they didn't choose and they cannot break free of the grip of manipulators. They are forced to lead the cruellest of lives, ones they rarely deserve.

My path led me to nervous breakdowns, mental hospitals, prison, destructive relationships, divorce, failing to be the best parent, failed businesses, poverty and homelessness. It was always one that I gravitated to in good mental health and in psychotic, hypermanic episodes, mine alone chosen by me.

The consequences of my path led to far harder, grimmer, and more gruelling realities at a time when I was a broken man, bested by the game of life. I was spent with no more left to give, collapsed on the wayside of my path, devoid of the purpose to travel forwards and yet torture came to me daily, like clockwork. After my bipolar diagnosis, I was given inhumane quantities of medication which destroyed my mind's ability to reason or lend perspective, raising my private castle in my skull-size kingdom to rubble, unable to see if my foundations were still intact at all, very, very scary indeed.

## Winning, waiting, winning and waiting

In the hands of mental health care professionals who all concurred that my daily dose was critical to its dual purpose, for others, the 'greater good' of every loved one's sanity and for me, a 'more likely' stable mental state in the end so that I could stand up again and continue my journey. This torturous win-wait gave instant satisfaction to everybody else but seemed so far in the distant and uncertain future to me that there was no light in my tunnel. Unable to see my path let alone the way or the horizon, daylight was as likely as the sun in parts of Norway at times of the year.

I languished on a diet of loss and failure for breakfast, hopelessness and shame for lunch, and obscene size helpings of guilt, regret, and remorse for dinner. This banquet was force-fed to me by me at a time when one spoonful made me mentally wretch. Yet somehow I held down all consumption and endured perpetual heartburn, unrelenting indigestion with a metaphorical incurable case of constipation.

And yet with all this said, I would not hesitate to explain that now in the present my eyes gazing adoringly at pictures of my beautiful children and supportive family, holding the hand of my partner, I have still had the good fortune of a charmed life and once more I am racing along the path with the sun on my face and the wind at my back. I have been lucky (self-made or gifted who knows) with far more events to smile about and to be proud of by a country mile.

Some experiences bear physical evidence like my graduation photo with my proud parents, but the majority are memories that are my valued private treasures, bringing me warmth and immense satisfaction. My mental recovery has kept all of these treasures intact. If anything they are clearer and more worthy than before. My journey has given me a strength forged in the fire of chaos and shaped by my will to endure it.

The capital 'T' of Truth is that with the biggest risks come the biggest rewards. We all fail in life, accept and embrace it. Nelson Mandela once said, 'There is nothing to be gained in life by playing small, nothing.' The American actor Denzel Washington said in a speech that 'to get something you never had you have to do something you have never done.' One of the biggest chances we take is on each other, and in my humble opinion it is always a chance worth taking, bonding makes us stronger.

## Hopes, fears, anxieties

From the very beginning of every human journey we connect with the world around us. People often gravitate to beautiful-looking people, but to bond you must be able to see the beauty within. At birth we all have that inner beauty plus the cutest features, the chubbiest hands and feet, and the biggest eyes, we all glow on the inside and we captivate our audience from their first sight of us. My personal experience at the birth of each of my children was euphoric to my spirit but tainted with the fear and anxiety in my mind. Material thoughts of making enough money to look after them as children, send them all to university, pay for their weddings, making me instantly afraid of the future. In a millisecond I calculated an additional 150,000 reasons to be scared stiff, overpowering the euphoric joy. I would recommend never thinking in these terms at the birth of any of your bundles of joy, I wish I'd been able to stay in the moment.

As a new life coming into the world, our spirit and beauty protect us from harm of most kinds, the fierce animal becomes the tame protector, the uglier the beast the more we see their beauty in their care for us. We have at this moment the most powerful new life force that is used for one purpose, our survival. I like to think that whoever becomes the selfless protector is given a bespoke and unique gift in return, somehow our new human spirit knows what gift is most needed and when to give it without the protector asking or expecting anything in return.

For some, it is the unseen gift of new lifeblood that repairs muscle and bone, replaces deficient DNA, and destroys harmful disease. For most of us, it is our minds that are in the most desperate need, replacing torment and guilt with a new peaceful purpose that satisfies our spirit in a fullness we cannot explain in any number of words, no matter how eloquent, carefully italicised or profound the linguistics they do not serve justice to it.

In every corner of our world, where there is new life, this miraculous sharing of gifts happens in the same way, of equal worth and without guidance or the need for maps or directions, simply the human spirit feeding one and another. We are all taught to understand the ritual of giving and receiving gifts, it is made clear in all cultures that giving has far greater virtue and value. To know the virtue of giving when forced by religious, community, or societal pressures serves as a righteous pat on the back, but the reward is hollow, nothing like the intrinsic reward of selfless giving. This is the best of humanity and the best part of us. Our hearts are open and our minds are free. Some men of letters will say that virtue rewards us as vice gives us punishment, only you can decide if this is true.

I leave you with a warning to keep your eyes open. There also exists the worst of us, evil deeds and evildoers that trade in harm and greed, unnatural and inhumane, selfish and cruel. They are the weakest of us all but wage the most harm and havoc, there is a void where there should be a strength of love and kindness, stolen by fear in the darkness and very rarely returned.

They will give their last morsel of food to us in our first years, but this is not a gift rather a shrewd investment for decades of return, nurturing these lives into future slaves to their control. For these, it is the receiving that they crave and hold dearest with constant greed for more.

## Spectres, chameleons and anglers of the mind

Most of us are lucky to have been born to good protectors of worth and merit but, even then, these spectres bide their time and may wait for us until adulthood. They are chameleons with the coldest blood, highly trained in the use of LOVE as their deception to the end game of control. Love is a sweet dream to most of the world but if caught by these forces it is a living and breathing nightmare. They will tear at your mental stability and are highly likely to make you feel physically and mentally unwell, over-and-over again.

They will use affection and perceived LOVE as they romance with great finesse, skilled anglers of mind manipulation with the sweetest of bait, the most delicate of hooks, and the finest silk nets to capture us in. For them love is performative, they plant a seed in the figment of your imagination to create blind faith and cold control. Most victims never return to the warm waters of life. Their performance is convincing with scripted scenes and acts of love, but these experiences are in the minority, the majority of their acts are full of poison that to the spectator speak the truth of their lies. Even a child would see the truth but, somehow, they hold down and cultivate their undeserving captives. The seed they plant grows a self-delusion in the hearts of their victims as they craft false decency and weave feelings into their performance.

In the game of life, on your path, some of you will experience both types of LOVE in one relationship, usually the good first and then over time maybe the ugly (bad, evil or otherwise) that is destructive and undeserved. If this misfortune ever happens to you I am truly sorry for your pain and suffering but I would beg of you to share your experience with your friends and family without reservation, and always remember none of this is your fault.

The very same can nearly always be said of your mental health, finding the joy in your life on your path is the education of a lifetime and it begins now, I wish you LOVE.

I wish you fortune, and way more than LUCK.

Also by Frankie Owens

Winner of a rare Koestler Trust Platinum Award

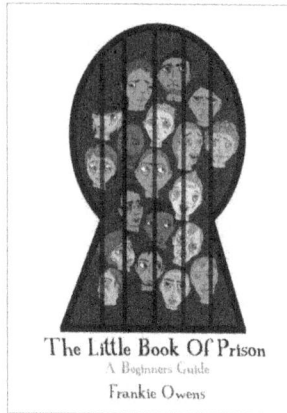

The Little Book Of Prison
A Beginners Guide
Frankie Owens

**The Little Book of Prison**
A Beginner's Guide

'This book is a winner on more than one level ... I was gripped from start to finish — roared with laughter one minute, winced with pain the next, and was left wondering why we have prisons at all'
*Tim Robertson, Chief Executive, The Koestler Trust.*

Paperback & ebook | ISBN 978-1-904380-83-2

www.WatersidePress.co.uk

# READ AND GROW

www.readandgrowsociety.org

All royalties from this book go to Read and Grow. Every copy sold helps adults learn to read. If you can't read, you can't grow.

Read and Grow is a voluntary group teaching local people to read.

The Read and Grow Society is as strong as the communities that are passionate about community literacy.

Together we can do more than we can alone.
Let's bring our abilities and passions together to affect real change now and for the future.

Enquiries: books@readandgrowsociety.org